IRELAND

IRELAND

1,001 Things You Need to Know

RICHARD KILLEEN

Atlantic Books
London

First published in Great Britain in 2017 by Atlantic Books,
an imprint of Atlantic Books Ltd.

1 2 3 4 5 6 7 8 9

A CIP catalogue record for this book is available
from the British Library.

Lines from 'Dublin' by Louis MacNeice, from *Selected Poems*,
Faber & Faber, 2007, reproduced by kind permission
of David Higham Associates Ltd.

Map artwork by Jeff Edwards

Hardback ISBN: 978-1-78649-158-9
E-book ISBN: 978-1-78649-1-596
Paperback ISBN: 978-1-78649-1-602

Printed in Great Britain by TJ International Ltd, Padstow, Cornwall

Atlantic Books
An Imprint of Atlantic Books Ltd
Ormond House
26–27 Boswell Street
London
WC1N 3JZ

www.atlantic-books.co.uk

This book is for Richard, my son.

Contents

This lovely land that always sent
Her writers and artists to banishment
And in a spirit of Irish fun
Betrayed her own leaders, one by one.
'Twas Irish humour, wet and dry,
Flung quicklime into Parnell's eye;*
'Tis Irish brains that save from doom
The leaky barge of the Bishop of Rome
For everyone knows the Pope can't belch
Without the consent of Billy Walsh.†

James Joyce, from *Gas From a Burner*

I live in Ireland by choice, after experience of living many
other places, and I am happy here. Our neighbours are
friendly, our view is beautiful, my political friends are
fine upstanding people, my political enemies fascinating
in their own way. I don't mind the gossip any more than
the rain. The censors are no longer eating writers in the
street. We are not as bad as we are painted, especially by
ourselves. In fact I love Ireland, as most Irish people do,
with only an occasional fit of the shudders.

Conor Cruise O'Brien, *States of Ireland* (1972)

What ish my nation? Ish a villain and
a bastard and a knave and a rascal.

The Irishman Macmorris in
Shakespeare, *Henry V*, act 3, scene 3

* An incident in a heated by-election campaign in 1891.
† The contemporary (1912) Archbishop of Dublin. Walsh is often pronounced
'Welsh' in Ireland, which makes the rhyme.

Acknowledgements

I am grateful to the staffs of the National Library of Ireland, the National Archives of Ireland and Dublin City Libraries. The press offices of the Gaelic Athletic Association and An Garda Síochána were efficient and helpful. My friends Pat Cooke, Sandra D'Arcy, Tony Farmar, Jennifer Brady, Michael Fewer, Andrea Martin, Terence Brown and Eric Dempsey all made helpful suggestions, provided me with information that I might have struggled to come by otherwise and corrected my mistakes. I appreciate the help and advice of my agent Ivan Mulcahy. It has been a pleasure to work with Will Atkinson and James Nightingale at Atlantic Books. Beth Humphries has been an exemplary and scrupulous copy-editor, for whose professionalism I am extremely grateful.

1

LAND, LANDSCAPE AND SOCIETY

Ireland at a Glance

Population: The 2016 census in the Republic of Ireland (ROI) recorded 4,747,976 persons in its preliminary results. The best current estimate (2016) for Northern Ireland (NI) is 1,851,600, split 46 per cent Protestant (effectively Unionist, wishing to remain in the UK) to 44 per cent Catholic (Nationalist, wishing – at least rhetorically – to join ROI). For the first time, the percentage of respondents declaring no religious affiliation has crept into double figures, if only just at 10 per cent. This narrowing of the traditional gap between the two religious affiliations is not progressive: while those who declare themselves Protestant are no longer the majority, there is no indication of a Catholic majority in the foreseeable future. There is what appears to be demographic deadlock.

Area: 84,421 sq. km / 32,595 square miles. That's a little smaller than the state of Maine but a bit bigger than that of West Virginia. Near enough, it's about the same size as South Carolina. In European terms, that makes the island about the same size as the Nouvelle-Aquitaine, the south-western region of France between Bordeaux and the Spanish border. It's a bit bigger than Bavaria, about the same size as Austria and about two-thirds the size of England. It's the third-largest island in Europe after Great Britain and Iceland and well ahead of all the Mediterranean islands.

Highest point: Carrantuohill, in the Macgillycuddy's Reeks in Co. Kerry, 1,038 metres/3,406 feet. Not exactly Alpine, but try climbing it in Irish weather. Actually, don't: it's very dangerous in bad weather.

Lowest point: North Slob, Co. Wexford, a wildfowl reserve that was created in the nineteenth century at the estuary of the River Slaney in the south-east of the island.

Most northerly point: Ballyhillin, Malin Head, Co. Donegal

Most southerly point: Brow Head, Mizen Peninsula, Co. Cork

Most westerly point: Dunmore Head, Dunquin, Co. Kerry

Most easterly point: Burr Point, Ards Peninsula, Co. Down

Length of coastline: 3,171 km / 1,970 miles

Furthest point from the sea: Close to the village of Lecarrow, Co. Roscommon

Largest lake: Lough Neagh, which borders five of the six counties of Northern Ireland (Co. Fermanagh being the exception), 383 sq. km / 148 sq. miles); the largest freshwater lake in the British Isles

Longest river: the Shannon, 386 km / 240 miles. It rises at Shannon Pot, Co. Cavan and with its tributaries, drains much of the centre of the island as it flows south and then west to enter the Atlantic between Co. Clare and Co. Kerry

Highest and lowest recorded temperatures: 33.3°C at Kilkenny, 26 June 1887; -19.1°C at Markree Castle, Co. Sligo, 16 January 1881

Principal economic activities: agriculture, information technology, financial services, medical and pharmaceutical

Numbers in education: (ROI) primary, 544,696; secondary, 372,296; tertiary, 173,649. The aggregate figure of 1,090,641 represents about 23 per cent of the ROI population in the education system. In NI, there are 168,669 pupils in primary schools; 141,112 in secondary; and 56,445 in tertiary. This represents just under 20 per cent of NI's population, although it does not account for NI students who attend third-level institutions in either ROI or Great Britain.

Divisions, Provinces and Counties

The island is partitioned under the terms of the Government of Ireland Act 1920, which began the process whereby the Act of Union of 1801 was unravelled. In its place, devolved government was established. The six north-eastern counties of Ulster, which had a local Protestant majority, wished to remain part of the United Kingdom, unlike the remaining twenty-six counties on the island which were overwhelmingly Catholic and which now comprise the Republic of Ireland.

There are four historic provinces: Ulster, having nine counties – six of which are in Northern Ireland (NI) and three in the Republic (ROI); Leinster, comprising twelve counties; Munster, six and Connacht five.

Ulster counties: Antrim, Down, Armagh, Londonderry, Tyrone, Fermanagh (NI), Cavan, Monaghan, Donegal (ROI)

Leinster counties: Dublin, Louth, Meath, Westmeath, Longford, Laois, Offaly, Carlow, Kilkenny, Wexford, Wicklow, Kildare

Munster counties: Cork, Kerry, Limerick, Tipperary, Waterford, Clare

Connacht counties: Galway, Mayo, Sligo, Leitrim, Roscommon

Principal Cities by Population
(urban area only)

Dublin	1,110,627
Belfast	483,418
Cork	198,582
Limerick	95,854

Derry	93,512
Galway	76,778

The most densely populated counties are Dublin and Antrim; the most sparsely populated is Co. Leitrim.

Nomenclature

The Roman geographer Ptolomy (fl. AD 150) called the island *Iouernia*, which is the likely root of the word Ireland. The more usual Latin word for Ireland was *Hibernia* (wintry land) which survives in the modern adjective Hibernian. In Old English or Anglo-Saxon, the word for the inhabitants of the island was *Iras*, the most likely root of the adjective Irish and possibly, by extension, of the word Ireland itself.

The Gaelic name is Éire, derived from Ériu, an ancient pre-Celtic goddess. Alternative poetic names – Banba and Fódla – derive from the names of similar goddesses.

World Heritage Sites

Brú na Bóinne, series of Bronze Age, pre-Celtic burial sites in Co. Meath, of which the most famous and most fully excavated is Newgrange

Skellig Michael, a spectacular triangular sea stack off the coast of Co. Kerry, a monastic anchorite site dating from the seventh century

Giant's Causeway, Co. Antrim, an area of about 40,000 hexagonal basalt columns on the northern Atlantic coast near the village of Bushmills

Other Sites of Outstanding Natural Beauty
(a personal list)

Torr Head, Co. Antrim is at the northern end of the beautiful Antrim Coast Road. You can drive up to the top and find yourself looking down on the Mull of Kintyre, for Scotland is barely 14 miles away across the North Channel.

Slea Head, Co. Kerry, at the western tip of the Dingle Peninsula. If you hug the tiny coast road to the village of Dunquin, you suddenly round a bend and there lie the Blasket islands offshore: the Great Blasket nearest and looking like a sleeping lion.

Glenmacnass, Co. Wicklow. The Wicklow Mountains, just to the south of Dublin, are not particularly high but they constitute a splendid wilderness. The British built a military road through these mountains after the 1798 rebellion, to help flush out fleeing rebels and to penetrate a region that had harboured them. Where the road begins the long drop into the valley of Glendalough, it bends left to avoid the Glenmacnass Waterfall. It's not the highest waterfall in the country: that's at Powerscourt in the same county; it drops 106 metres/350 feet and is the third tallest in the British Isles. But Glenmacnass, with its view down the valley, is the more dramatic.

Lough Cullin, Co. Mayo, of which the author Desmond Fennell wrote: 'The sunlight, falling from an unsettled sky, showed the water luminous and leaden, and a patch of hillside very green. Then the light moved over the hillside and a touch of blue appeared in the lake. It was like a shot being set up for some celestial camera. With that surprise which Irish people sometimes experience when they travel in Ireland, I understood why an Englishman or a German, coming here to fish, would think this paradise.'

Slieve League, Co. Donegal. The sea cliffs here are the tallest on the Irish mainland at 601 metres/1,972 feet. The cliffs at Croaghaun on Achill Island are taller but there is no viewing or vantage point. The Cliffs of Moher in Co. Clare are more famous but it's Slieve League for me – and for many others. While size may not be everything, it's worth noting that the height of the Eiffel Tower is 324 metres/1,063 feet.

Lough Derg, Co. Tipperary. This is the largest lake in the Shannon system and is best seen from a viewing point on the R494 road between Nenagh, Co. Tipperary and Killaloe, Co. Clare. The viewing point is just beyond the village of Portroe.

Best Beaches
(a personal list)

Inch, Co. Kerry
Curracloe, Co. Wexford
North Bull Island, Dublin
Keem Bay, Achill Island, Co. Mayo
Gurteen Bay, Co. Galway
Inchydoney, Co. Cork
Brittas Bay, Co. Wicklow
Magheroarty, Co. Donegal
Mulranny, Co. Mayo
Laytown & Bettystown, Co. Meath

Ten Longest Rivers

---

	km
Shannon	360
Barrow	192

Suir	184
Blackwater	168
Bann	159
Nore	140
Suck	133
Liffey	132
Erne	129
Foyle	129

Highest Mountains

The Macgillycuddy's Reeks in Co. Kerry contain the eight highest mountains in Ireland, ranging from Carrantuohill (1,038 metres/ 3,406 ft) to Cruach Mhór (932/3,058). The remaining ten highest peaks, other than those in the Reeks, are as follows:

		metres / feet
Mount Brandon	Dingle Peninsula, Co. Kerry	951 / 3,120
Lugnaquilla	Co. Wicklow	925 / 3,035
Galtymore	Co. Tipperary	917 / 3,009
Slieve Donard	Co. Down	852 / 2,795
Baurtregaum	Dingle Peninsula, Co. Kerry	851 /2,792
Mullaghcleevaun	Co. Wicklow	849 / 2,785
Mangerton	Co. Kerry	839 / 2,753
Caherconree	Co. Kerry	835 / 2,740
Purple Mountain	Co. Kerry	832 / 2,730
Beenoskee	Co. Kerry	826 / 2,710

In short, Co. Kerry is well supplied with mountains.

Ten Most Common Native Trees

Oak	Aspen
Elm	Willow
Birch	Rowan
Alder	Whitebeam
Cherry	Crab apple

Most Common Birds of Ireland

RESIDENT SPECIES

Chaffinch	Jackdaw
Robin	Rook
Wren	Blackbird
Dunnock	Starling
Wood pigeon	Magpie

WINTER VISITORS

Dunlin	Fieldfare
Knot	Black-tailed godwit
Wigeon	Brent goose
Teal	Scaup
Redwing	Lapwing

SUMMER VISITORS

Swallow	Sand martin
Willow warbler	Common tern
Chiffchaff	Storm petrel
Sedge warbler	Arctic tern
House martin	Sandwich tern

Ten Most Common Irish Mammals

Fox	Badger
Hedgehog	Hare
Stoat	Deer
Otter	Pine marten
Pygmy shrew	Rabbit

Bogs and The Burren

About 5 per cent of the island is bogland, formed by dead plants decomposing and compressing over millennia in the wet Irish climate. There are two types: blanket bogs which are generally shallow and found on mountainsides that attract heavy rainfall; and larger bogs, mainly found in the midlands, which are 'raised' and flat, having a depth of up to eight metres. These are the bogs that can be harvested for fuel in the form of peat briquettes for domestic heating together with ancillary products that can be used as fertilizers.

As with any other unique habitat, the bogs are home to wild flora that are seldom if ever found in other locales. A similar condition affects the remarkable karst landscape of Co. Clare known as the Burren (p. 169) which is host to alpine flora found nowhere else in Ireland (or most other places in north-west Europe).

Most Common Native Irish Plants

Broom	Dog rose	Wild cherry
Bird cherry	Elder	Ragged Robin
Aspen	Strawberry tree	

2

PEOPLE

From pre-Celts to Polish plumbers

Pre-Celts

Of these peoples, we know almost nothing. We don't know what they looked like or what languages they spoke or where they originated. Gaelic mythology later proposed a succession of invading peoples but until the Celts themselves arrived around 300 BC and overran the island all is conjecture. But we know that there was a long history of pre-Celtic settlement. The oldest archaeological site is at Mount Sandel, Co. Londonderry, near the mouth of the River Bann. It has been dated to 5935 BC. Then there is the Boyne Valley complex in Co. Meath, centred on Newgrange, which dates from about 2500 BC.

Newgrange is a large circular cairn, more than 100 metres in diameter, containing a central burial chamber. It was built with the greatest care and skill. The roofing stones were provided with shallow, concave channels to act as gutters, carrying rainwater to the outside of the cairn and away from the burial chamber. Most famous is the carefully positioned light box over the entrance, aligned so that on the morning of the winter solstice – and on that morning only – the rays of the rising sun penetrate the full distance of the passage into the burial chamber itself.

The Neolithic people who built this extraordinary structure were not just simple farmers. They were skilled in construction techniques, in lapidary design and in astronomical observation.

Celts

The word Celt is used rather loosely, not least by English people who badge the other three nations of the British Isles as Celtic. This is inaccurate, or at least exaggerated, in respect of Ireland and Scotland although it has more merit with reference to Wales. Basically, Celtic denotes a pair of linguistic divisions. The so-called

P-Celtic languages are Welsh, Cornish and Breton; the Q-Celtic languages are Irish, Scots Gaelic and Manx. Both are descended from a lost Ur-Celtic language. By extension, the word Celt is then used as an ethnic category to describe countries where these languages are – or once were – spoken. That's where the problem lies: the word properly describes a language group, not an ethnic one.

The Celts were a central European Iron Age people whose migrations covered much of the continent. In Britain, they were displaced by the Angles and Saxons and pushed west into what is now Wales. They first arrived in Ireland around 300 BC. Successive waves of Celtic invaders overran the island, completely obliterating or absorbing the existing population. The last of the major Celtic groups to arrive were the *Gaeil* and it was they who effectively took possession of the entire island. It is from them that we get the word Gaelic.

Unlike in Britain, they remained undisturbed by foreign invasion for almost 1,000 years. In the fifth century AD, they adopted Christianity. Gaelic Ireland was a pastoral, warlord society with no central government or capital city. Indeed, there were no towns or cities at all. But there was a common language, a common legal system, and a common currency based on the value of cattle. It was not remotely egalitarian. Rather it was highly stratified, with regional or local kings at the top along with lawyers and poets. The latter were important because they memorized royal genealogies.

Late Gaelic Ireland, up to the end of the eighth century, was one of the beacons of Western Christianity at a time when the continent was still recovering from the collapse of the Roman Empire. However, Ireland's happy isolation could not last for ever; the wonder is that it lasted as long as it did. When it was eventually disturbed, it was at the hands of violent seaborne warriors from Scandinavia.

The Vikings

Viking raiders first appeared off the east coast of Ireland in 795, less than a decade after their first attack on Britain. Irish monasteries, with their precious ornaments and vessels, offered tempting targets. Over time, the raids increased and the Vikings established trading settlements, which gradually developed into the first Irish towns. Dublin's foundation date is 841. Wexford, Waterford, Cork and Limerick are likewise all of Viking foundation.

Such permanent settlements meant displacing local Gaelic sub-kings and naturally invited counter-attack. The tenth and eleventh centuries saw a pattern of intermittent warfare between Vikings and Gaels. Occasionally Vikings allied themselves with one side or the other in a dispute between Gaelic warlords. This pattern reached its peak in 1014 at the Battle of Clontarf, on the north shore of Dublin Bay. This was a kind of Gaelic civil war in which Brian Ború – the effective ruler of the southern half of the island – was attempting to assert his claim to the high kingship of the entire island. Both Brian and those resisting him had Viking allies to assist them. Brian won a Pyrrhic victory, at the cost of his own life, but thereafter the island reverted to its traditional chequerboard of provincial kingdoms and sub-kingdoms. There was no insular unity.

The Vikings left an indelible mark on Ireland by establishing its first towns and developing its early structures of seaborne commerce. Their legacy is also there in place names – Leixlip near Dublin, for example, means salmon leap. Even more so, it's there in surnames. The common Irish surname Doyle is derived from the Gaelic *dubh ghaill* meaning dark foreigner, a reference to the dark-haired Danes as distinct from the fair-haired Norwegians. That said, the Viking impact was nothing compared to what came next.

The Normans

The Normans were the descendants of Vikings who had settled in what is now Normandy in north-west France and were vassals of the King of France. As the world knows, they conquered England in 1066. In 1169, a Norman invasion force came to Ireland at the invitation of the provincial king of Leinster, who had lost his kingdom in a matrimonial dispute and needed military muscle to recover it. This was provided by a body of Normans based in Wales. Their military superiority soon established and consolidated their position, especially in the south-eastern quadrant.

In the wake of the Normans came continental developments in architecture, in the spread of new religious orders, in new legal systems and the further development of towns. Most fatefully of all, it inserted the royal power of England into Irish affairs. King Henry II was so concerned that Norman success might lead to the establishment of an independent kingdom on his western flank that he came to Ireland in 1171 with a formidable military force and accepted the submission of the Norman colonists and most of the Gaelic kings as well. Ireland was now deemed to be a lordship of the English crown.

The effect of the Norman presence has been permanent and profound. It is clearly visible to this day. The Normans never conquered the entire island, although they were extremely good at settling themselves on the most fertile land. Throughout the medieval period, Norman lordships coexisted with Gaelic kingdoms in a see-saw relationship in which neither side ever totally dominated the other. It was into this world that the next significant group inserted themselves in the middle of the sixteenth century.

The New English

King Henry VIII's religious break with Rome and his urge towards greater centralization were inextricably mixed up. In the 1530s, he broke the magnate power of the greatest Hiberno-Norman family, the Fitzgeralds of Kildare. In 1541, he abolished the lordship and established Ireland as a separate but sister kingdom. In the wake of this there came to Ireland a new cohort of governors, administrators and military men whose aim was a more complete conquest of Ireland for the crown.

These are known to history as the New English. Their most distinctive characteristic was their Protestantism, for the Reformation failed in Ireland: Normans (now called Old English to distinguish them from the new interlopers) and Gaels alike remained Catholic. The next century brought a series of wars together with plantations of New English on conquered Irish lands until the final, complete English conquest of Ireland under Cromwell in the 1650s. There then followed a massive dispossession of Catholic landowners and their replacement by further New English planters, whose descendants would in time become known as the Protestant Ascendancy. But first, we need to back-track a little to the early 1600s and the Plantation of Ulster.

Ulster Protestants

Ulster was the province least penetrated by the Normans. In the face of ever-expanding English power under Elizabeth I, the Gaelic lords of Ulster rebelled in 1593 and, despite Spanish military aid, were finally defeated ten years later. The principal Ulster chiefs, O'Neill of Tyrone and O'Donnell of Donegal, fled to the continent. Their vast lands were forfeit to the crown and a huge plantation scheme – by far the biggest yet – was effected. The planters were all

Protestant, although there was an important distinction between English Anglicans and Scots Presbyterians, a distinction still visible today.

So Ulster went from being the most to the least Gaelic province in the course of a century. It had always been a distinct place and it was now marked off by religious and ethnic differences from the three southern provinces.

The Protestant Ascendancy

The term did not come into use until the 1790s but it describes the ruling elite descended from the Cromwellian land plantation. The ascendancy were not just Protestant – they were Anglican. The Church of Ireland, an Anglican sister of the Church of England, was established by law and only those conforming to it could sit in parliament, vote or enter the higher professions. Final Catholic resistance – by now the distinction between Gaels and Old English had been elided if not quite eliminated – was only overcome in the 1690s.

From then until the late nineteenth century, the ascendancy were the key power in the land. In common with all contemporary dominant religious groups, they discriminated against other confessions, in this case Catholics and Dissenters. The disabilities were more severe in the former than the latter. What made Ireland unusual, however, was that the ascendancy were a minority rather than a majority group. They constituted barely 10 per cent of the Irish population. The contrast with contemporary England and France was stark: there, legal disabilities were directed by a confessional majority against dissenting minorities. In Ireland, it was the other way round.

What does Ireland owe the ascendancy? Most visibly, the wonderful Georgian architecture of Dublin and other cities together with some magnificent country houses. Being Anglo-Irish, they facilitated the gradual spread of the English language and the retreat of Irish, although the disastrous famine of the mid nineteenth century accelerated that process. The various institutions of higher learning and scholarship were largely an ascendancy preserve until the twentieth century.

A series of Land Acts in the last quarter of the nineteenth century gradually saw the break-up of the ascendancy estates and the replacement of the landlords by a new class of owner-proprietors, who had previously been tenants. These are the modern Irish farming class.

Recent Immigrants

The huge expansion of the Irish economy from the early 1990s to the financial and property collapse of 2008 turned Ireland from a nation of emigrants to one of immigrants. In particular, free movement of people within the EU facilitated the arrival of many from the eastern accession states. There was at one stage a weekly bus service between Warsaw and Dublin. Many worked in the construction boom until the crash. The more footloose left as the construction industry contracted violently but those who were married – and especially those who had children in the school system – had a strong incentive to stay. As I write (2016) it is still a commonplace to find Poles, Lithuanians, Croats and even Russians working in bars and restaurants. They are the New Irish.

TEN IMMIGRANTS WHO MADE A DIFFERENCE

St Patrick(s)	the national apostle(s)
Sitric Silkenbeard	Norse King of Dublin who founded Christ Church Cathedral (1038)
William Marshall (c.1146–1219)	consolidated the Norman conquest of Ireland

Sir William Davies	key member of the New English elite: attorney-general and speaker of the Irish parliament (early 17th century)
Richard Boyle, 1st Earl of Cork (1566–1643)	dynast and New English adventurer
Sir Arthur Chichester (1563–1625)	promoter of the Ulster Plantation; founder of Belfast
James Gandon (1742–1823)	principal architect of Georgian Dublin
Samuel Louis Crommelin (1652–1717)	founder of the Ulster linen industry
Maud Gonne (1866–1953)	revolutionary and muse of W.B. Yeats
Thom McGinty (1952–95)	The Diceman, beloved Dublin street artist, self-styled stillness artist and human statue

3
NATIONAL CHARACTERISTICS

In general, this is a dubious area – for two reasons. First, what are called national characteristics are more often national caricatures projected on to a community by outsiders (thus parsimonious Scots, sexually inept English, Welsh men not to be left alone with sheep). Second, even to the extent that some characteristics may be more or less true, they can change over time. What follows in this section comes with a mixture of scepticism and levity.

Eloquence: the Gift of the Gab

> The English hoard words like misers. The Irish
> spend them like drunken sailors.
>
> Kenneth Tynan

You might be forgiven for thinking that this is a myth if you spent time listening to debates in the Dáil, the lower house of the Irish parliament. The standard of debate is often lamentable and very few of the deputies would ever be suspected of kissing the Blarney Stone. This practice, in which a person is held upside down by the heels to kiss part of the stonework on Blarney Castle in Co. Cork, is reputed to convey the gift of eloquence. It is very popular with tourists.

The myth arose because it was alleged that the owner of Blarney Castle in the early seventeenth century, Cormac McCarthy, bamboozled the New English Lord President of Munster, Sir George Carew, with a tissue of loquacious lies and half-truths. Thereafter, blarney became a generic term for every kind of Irish evasion and blather.

Visitors to Ireland comment on the quick verbal dexterity of Irish people. Is this the myth becoming a sort of self-fulfilling prophecy, as if expecting the gift of the gab is enough to conjure it into life? Not necessarily. There is a sharpness of expression and a weakness for whimsy and improbable simile that is sometimes impossible to miss. Overheard in a Dublin pub, as an American visitor signals to the barman for his bill: Barman, 'You want the bill, sir?' American (cheerfully), 'We call it the check.' Barman, 'Well, you're not in the Check Republic now.'

This sort of thing is not unique to Dublin or to Ireland. I have heard repartee just as quick as that in London or New York. But visitors find it more ubiquitous in Ireland and comment on it as something characteristic of the country. This can't all be self-fulfilling prophecy; it must have some evidential basis, even if the evidence can be a bit stretched or exaggerated at times.

And it's supported by a body of literature that depends to an exceptional extent on verbal ingenuity. Joyce's *Ulysses* is, of course, the gold standard but his successors, Beckett and Flann O'Brien, are of the same school. It's there in Anglo-Irish fiction too, not least in the character of Flurry Knox. He appears in Somerville and Ross's *Some Experiences of an Irish RM*, in which an English resident magistrate in rural Ireland is outwitted and gulled by Knox, the local Master of Foxhounds. Knox is no shifty peasant but a member of the ascendancy, yet his conduct is little different and depends similarly on lots of blarney. And of all the fine arts, literature – words, words, words – is the one where Ireland has consistently out-performed all reasonable expectations based on population. Four Nobel Prizes and none of them for Joyce!

Alcohol: One for the Road and Then One for the Ditch

Ireland has a reputation for heavy alcohol consumption and it's one that is supported by the evidence. According to the World Atlas (worldatlas.com, February 2017), Ireland is seventh in the world in the consumption of alcohol, measured in litres per capita. That sounds not too bad, until you look at who is above it. Gold, silver and bronze in the booze Olympics go to Estonia, Belarus and Lithuania. Then comes tiny Andorra, the Czech Republic and Austria. So ignoring Andorra – so small as to be statistically irrelevant – Ireland has the second-highest consumption rate among countries that never suffered from Soviet occupation.

Alcohol plays a prominent role in Irish literature. One whole episode (chapter) of *Ulysses* and part of another are set in pubs. In the first instance, the anonymous narrator of the Cyclops episode cadges a pint and then declares: 'Ah! Ow! Don't be talking! I was blue mouldy for the want of that pint. Declare to God I could hear it hit the pit of my stomach with a click.' Earlier in the novel, in the Lestrygonians episode, Leopold Bloom contents himself with a chaste lunchtime repast of a Gorgonzola sandwich and a glass of burgundy in Davy Byrne's pub in Duke Street, which happily is still in business. In his masterpiece, *At Swim-Two-Birds*, Flann O'Brien invents a character called Jem Casey, the poet of the pick, who composes a piece of doggerel in praise of plain porter: 'A Pint of Plain is Your Only Man'. Moreover, booze courses like a leitmotif through that book, perhaps foreshadowing O'Brien's eventual collapse into hopeless alcoholism.

Which is, of course, where the picture darkens. Alcoholism and heavy drinking has been an historic problem in Ireland, to the extent that it has spawned two major temperance campaigns. In the 1840s, Fr Theobald Mathew's campaign for teetotalism won huge national support under the slogan 'Ireland Sober is Ireland Free'. In the post-Famine years from the 1850s on, the movement weakened. But in 1898, another priest, Fr James Cullen SJ, founded the Pioneer Total Abstinence Association. It gained a huge following. By the 1950s, its membership was not far short of 500,000 people – that in a country whose total population at the time was just under 3 million. In common with other Catholic initiatives, it succumbed to the gradual erosion of religious allegiance from the 1960s on and it is now rare to see anyone wearing the distinctive Pioneer lapel badge.

None the less, secular efforts have continued to combat the demon drink. None have been so successful – albeit the success is incomplete – as that directed at tackling the drink-driving problem. This has effected a major change in social behaviour. Combined with a ban on smoking in public places, it has had a seriously damaging impact on rural pubs. The *Irish Independent* newspaper, the country's top-selling daily, estimates that about 1,000 pubs have closed in Ireland in ten years, although how much of this is attributable to the drink-driving campaign and how much to the post-2008 recession is unknown. Still, the remaining 7,500 pubs serve a total population (ROI and NI) of barely 6 million. So Paddy isn't going to die of thirst just yet.

A Nation of Readers

> A boy of your age, he [the narrator's uncle] said at last, who gives himself up to the sin of sloth – what in God's name is going to happen to him when he goes out to face the world? Boys but I often wonder what the world is coming to. I do indeed. Tell me this, do you ever open a book at all?
>
> Flann O'Brien, *At Swim-Two-Birds*

It was a belief firmly embraced by Irish people and often repeated, on no evidence whatsoever, by visitors that the Irish bought books in disproportionate numbers compared to other countries. Alas, it is not so. The Irish buy books in numbers broadly comparable to those in other first-world countries with universal literacy. A survey in 2002 found that 42 per cent of people had read no book in the preceding year and that 68 per cent of all books had been read by 24 per cent of the population. This is broadly in line with international experience.

The myth of exceptional Irish book-buying and reading probably arose because of the outstanding achievements of Irish literature. It is a legitimate source of national pride, although – ironically – it had to coexist for many years with one of the most draconian literary censorship regimes in the developed world. One theory that may have helped the myth to form arose from the misinterpretation of a household survey on book expenditure which bundled school books in with all the rest.

At any rate, a properly scientific survey in 1987, commissioned by the Irish Books Marketing Group, finally exploded the myth. Worse again, the survey found that only 33 per cent of Irish adults claimed to be reading a book at the time, a figure lower than that for the UK or the US but (surprise, surprise) higher than that for France.

Anti-English

'The curse of a goodfornothing God light side sideways on the bloody thicklugged sons of whores' gets! No music and no art and no literature worthy of the name. Any civilisation they have they stole from us. Tonguetied sons of bastards' ghosts.'

Thus the ridiculous comic character in Joyce's *Ulysses* known simply as The Citizen, venting his summary of the English and their virtues. It is precisely the comic exaggeration of this and similar passages that registers its absurdity, the embittered ravings of a cadger and a soak. Whatever The Citizen was, he was representative of no one but himself.

The idea that the Irish dislike the English contains just enough truth to keep it feebly alive, but on the whole it is quite untrue. As in any country, there is a minority of xenophobes who dislike foreigners – and England, in Irish eyes, is the biggest foreigner of all. In this, the Irish are little different from the Scots and the Welsh. England is the big boy on the block and the richest. That's bound to cause resentment among those who enjoy resenting.

But the plain fact is that the British Isles possess, to a large degree, a common culture – albeit with important regional variations. Anyone visiting from overseas can see the signs of that common culture: suburban housing patterns; steering wheels on the right and traffic on the left; fish and chips; the English language. To a French or German eye, all these things and many others are different to their own arrangements and are among the things that are characteristic of Britain and Ireland.

Ireland is part of that difference. We love fish and chips, double-decker buses and the Premiership. We love our suburban houses with gardens front and back. We don't like the idea of renting or living in apartments – although that is changing under the pressure of economics. Incidents of anglophobia are vanishingly rare, as any English tourist can testify. So where does this idea come from, that the Irish dislike the English?

Well, as with everything in Ireland, history plays a part. English rule in Ireland was illegitimate and increasingly regarded as such. But once independence was secured for most of the island, that boil was lanced. As for Northern Ireland, only the deluded believe that London is selfishly holding on to NI rather than that the local population has bitterly divided national loyalties. London would be out of NI in the morning if it could.

So what's left? Well, it's back to that big boy on the block syndrome. Everyone else likes to see him tripped up now and again. Sport provides the perfect context. I remember watching an England–France football international in a crowded pub once, when England, having led 1–0 for most of the game, conceded two late goals. The whole place went wild, everyone there having been shouting frantically for the French. Well, all except one. He was English and had lived here happily for some years but suddenly felt a long way from home. He was thoroughly miserable – but then he was from Yorkshire. And that's about as bad and as harmless as it gets. The Yorkshire lad had his leg pulled unmercifully but was consoled by having pints bought for him for the rest of the evening.

Mad for Sport

'For the honour of the little village... for the honour of the old home.'

Matt the Thresher in Knocknagow
by Charles Kickham (1869)

Now there is no doubting this one. Sport is a huge factor in Irish life. Gaelic games, principally football and hurling, are the most popular. They are organized under the aegis of the Gaelic Athletic Association (GAA), a mostly voluntary body that has a presence in every corner of Irish life – except among Ulster Protestants, who generally avoid it as being too nationalist. It has just over 1,600 affiliated clubs in all, with a presence in every county in Ireland. The GAA estimates that the number of people who either play the games or coach and manage or administrate is between 500,000 and 600,000. The Association is organized on a county basis by a county board which sends delegates to an annual national congress.

Moreover, the GAA has developed an international reach. It always had a presence among the Irish-American diaspora. But now there are 64 affiliated clubs in Australia, 22 scattered across East Asia, 111 in North America and 71 across Europe. The latter are administered by the quaintly named European County Board.

Gaelic football is the most popular sport in Ireland. It is played in every county in the island. Its national championship is organized on a provincial basis, with the provincial champions going forward to All-Ireland quarter finals. From then on, it's knockout. The final is played in mid-September in the GAA's showpiece headquarters, Croke Park in Dublin, before a full house of 82,300. 'Croker' is one of the five biggest stadiums in Europe.

The GAA was founded in 1884 to revive the ancient Irish game of hurling. This is a stick and ball game and is reckoned to be the fastest field game in the world. At its best, it is a magnificent spectacle, requiring courage, speed and astonishing skill. But the GAA's foundation ambition has not been fulfilled, because hurling is really a regional rather than a national pastime. It has no serious presence in the northern half of the island above the Dublin–Galway line, except for a few pockets in east Ulster – especially in the Glens of Antrim.

Even then, no county team from above that line has ever won the All-Ireland Senior Hurling championship. Antrim has occasionally reached the final – the last time was in 1989 – only to lose. The strongest hurling counties are these:

Kilkenny	Waterford
Tipperary	Limerick
Cork	Wexford
Clare	Galway

Of these, the first three have won more than 75 per cent of all championships since the inaugural year of 1887. It is worth noting that all of them except Galway have a county border touching one of the others. Even then, Galway has a county border with the small midland county of Offaly which produced some remarkable teams from slender resources in the 1980s and '90s and won two championships in each of those decades.

As in every country, Association Football (soccer) is hugely popular, with participation rates very high. The domestic senior competitions both in ROI and NI are, however, poorly – although passionately – supported; they live in the shadow of the English Premiership, with all its bling, money and showbiz glamour. Premiership replica shirts are more frequently seen on Irish streets than those of even the biggest domestic clubs. The English clubs with the biggest Irish following are Manchester United (inevitably), Liverpool and Arsenal; it is commonplace to hear fans refer to their clubs proprietorially in the first person plural.

Rugby Union has advanced by leaps and bounds in Ireland since the game went professional in the mid 1990s. In particular, spectator numbers have increased dramatically, as the four provincial teams have reinvented themselves as professional franchises. Ulster has won the premier European trophy once, Munster twice and Leinster three times in what was a golden era from 1999 to 2012. These successes have come at some cost to the club game, however; inevitably the focus has been on the professional game at provincial and national level.

The international team is chosen on an all-Ireland basis and has had mixed success over the years. Ireland has always produced outstanding players but sometimes not enough of them at the same time. It has only won two grand slams – defeating all opponents in the Six- (formerly Five-) Nations' Championship – in 1949 and 2009.

Horse racing is another Irish passion; indeed, the love affair with the horse is of long standing in Ireland. There are 26 major courses, two of them in NI. The principal meetings are the Irish Derby meeting at The Curragh, Co. Kildare; the Irish Grand National meeting over the Easter weekend in Fairyhouse, Co. Meath; and the Punchestown, Co. Kildare spring National Hunt meeting. The four-day Galway Races festival in late July is a national attraction, with the Listowel, Co. Kerry, festival in late September not far behind. It was said of Listowel that the punters comprised bank clerks trying to look drunk and parish priests trying to look sober. But probably the biggest event in the Irish racing calendar does not take place in Ireland at all but in Gloucestershire. Every March, there is a huge Irish exodus to the National Hunt Festival in Cheltenham.

Of the other sports, the one that bears some mention is golf. Ireland is blessed with some outstanding championship links courses. The best two, by general consent, are Portmarnock on the northern margins of Dublin and Royal Co. Down in NI.

The Craic: Round the House and Mind the Dresser

A criminal trial in the UK many years ago concerned a successful betting coup pulled off on an English racecourse by a small group of Irish rogues. After they had been convicted, the judge asked the leader of the syndicate, a Cork man, why they had done it. He replied 'For the craic.' The judge said 'For the what?' 'Ah, for the fun, man, the fun.'

Although the word hasn't made it to my 1993 edition of the *Shorter Oxford English Dictionary*, it is included in the latest edition of the *Oxford Spelling Dictionary*, where it is simply glossed as 'a good time'. That's as good a definition as any.

The term can cover a multitude and it is a state of mind as much as anything else. It's not as if other countries don't have fun. It's just a peculiarly Irish take on a universal impulse. The best place to encounter the craic is in a West of Ireland pub on a summer's evening, with local musicians playing traditional music and – best of all – an impromptu ceili in full swing. You won't mistake it for anywhere else.

Ten Quotes that are Close to the Bone

Brendan Behan: 'The first item on every Irish agenda is the Split.'

Hugh Leonard: 'Ireland will be very nice when it's finished.'

Samuel Johnson: 'The Irish are a fair people: they never speak well of one another.'

Winston Churchill: 'We have always found the Irish a bit odd. They refuse to be English.'

Oscar Wilde: 'I am Irish by race but the English have condemned me to talk the language of Shakespeare.'

Spike Milligan: 'Many people die of thirst but the Irish are born with one.'

Sigmund Freud: '[The Irish] is one race of people for whom psychoanalysis is no use whatsoever.'

Roddy Doyle: 'We have sold the myth of Dublin as a sexy place incredibly well because it's a dreary little dump most of the time.'

James Joyce: 'Oh Ireland, my first and only love – where Christ and Caesar are hand in glove.'

Conor Cruise O'Brien: 'Irishness is not a question of birth or blood or language: it is the condition of being involved in the Irish situation, and usually of being mauled by it.'

4

HEROES AND VILLAINS

Cú Chulainn (Cúchulainn)

The greatest hero of ancient Irish mythology, his narrative echoes that of many heroic figures in other oral traditions. Moreover, his story has served as a symbol or metaphor for modern Irish nationalism, as we shall see.

His name translates as the Hound of Culann. This Culann was a smith whose savage hound was slain by a remarkable young boy called Sétanta, who thereafter adopted the name Cú Chulainn. In remorse for killing the dog, which had been the smith's protector, Cú Chulainn now pledged himself to assume that role. By extension, he became the heroic warrior protecting an entire people from their enemies.

He is central to the canon of heroic tales and sagas of pre-Christian Celtic Ireland known collectively as the Ulster Cycle. It is so called because the people it concerns were known as the Ulaidh, from which the modern provincial name derives. The central saga in the cycle is the *Táin Bó Cuailnge* or Cattle Raid of Cooley. This tells of an attempt by Queen Méabh (Maeve) of Connacht to carry off a bull sacred to the Ulaidh. Her raiding army includes some renegade Ulster warriors who had quarrelled with Conchobhar, the northern king.

Single handed, Cú Chulainn slowed and impeded the invasion force. One by one, he engages the Connacht champions in single combat and defeats them all, culminating in the slaying of Ferdia, his beloved foster-brother. The army of the Ulaidh, roused from its torpor by Cú Chulainn's heroism, bestirs itself, mobilizes and defeats the Connacht army. As with all such mythical heroes, Cú Chulainn was invested with supernatural abilities which placed him outside nature. His death in battle while still young also follows a common trope. Knowing that death was near, he tied himself to a tree so that he might die on his feet.

As a symbol of heroic resistance against overwhelming odds, it is not hard to see the appeal of the Cú Chulainn legend to militant

Irish nationalists, faced as they were with what seemed the might of the British Empire. Patrick Pearse (see below) was a particular devotee of the Cú Chulainn legend and may even have regarded himself as a sort of spiritual reincarnation of the mythical hero. At any rate, the best-remembered leader of the Easter Rising of 1916 is symbolically recalled in bronze in the General Post Office, Dublin, the centre of the Rising. Oliver Sheppard's *The Death of Cuchulain* stands there today in commemoration of that transformative event.

In 'The Statues', one of his last poems, Yeats makes the connection explicit: 'When Pearse summoned Cuchulain to his side, / What stalked through the Post Office? What intellect, / What calculation, number, measurement, replied?'

St Patrick

According to the ballad, St Patrick was a gentleman – he came of dacent [sic] people. True. He is for the most part a figure of mystery, although the shadow of the real person is discernible. And this is for a reason: he is the first figure in the history of the island to leave us a written record of any kind. In his case, he has left us a record of himself, a kind of displaced autobiography.

Two fragments are all we have, but they are undoubtedly the work of his hand. So, who was he? He was the son of a Romanized British family, born in the early fifth century, who had been captured at the age of 16 by pirate raiders from Ireland and sold into slavery. His family was Christian, like all the late Roman elite, metropolitan and provincial alike. After six years, he eventually escaped back to Britain, but dreamed that he was being recalled to Ireland to evangelize the island for Christ.

He was probably not the first Christian missionary in the country but he was certainly one of the most potent. His mission appears to have been confined to the northern half of the island: the southern half contains no verifiable Patrician sites. And the two documents he has left us? The first, and more important, his *Confessio*, is the text from which we can patch together the outline of his life. It was not written to explain his life, rather to justify his mission against some who had questioned it. The second, the *Letter to Coroticus*, is a bitter protest against the depredations of a British chieftain whose troops came ashore in Ireland and slaughtered newly evangelized Christians, an outrage that Patrick must have felt with particular keenness given his own earlier experience at the hands of the Irish.

The most famous story of his mission has him standing on the Hill of Slane, to the north-west of Dublin, demonstrating the mystery of the Trinity to the local sub-king. The means used by Patrick to explain the Trinitarian nature of the Christian God was to show how a shamrock was a unity despite its trefoil leaf. It worked; the king converted.

Almost certainly, this yarn is the purest myth and there isn't a shred of evidence in support of it. Which is important: because the point of Patrick is not that we can prove he did this or that, or even that he was the national evangelist, but that he was the first living, breathing human being on the island of Ireland of whom we have a secure record, however tentative. Before Patrick, all is conjecture, heroic myth and uncertainty. Here is flesh and blood, a real person.

The arrival date for the beginning of Patrick's mission has traditionally been given as AD 432. Such evidence as we have points more plausibly to the later fifth century. There was another missionary, confusingly called Palladius, and his mission is dated to 431. This date is accepted by scholars as accurate. The Patrician date of 432 seems to have been an attempt – in the seventh century – to conflate the two missions into one.

This may have been part of an attempt by the see of Armagh to establish its primacy in the early Irish Church. Claiming Patrick – whose associations with Armagh appear to have been many – as the sole national evangelist, meant that the development of his cult could only assist Armagh's primatial ambitions. At any rate, the cult developed and Armagh's primacy was eventually confirmed by the Pope in the early twelfth century. It retains that status today. As for Patrick, his grave is reputed to be in the grounds of Down Cathedral in Downpatrick, not far from Armagh.

Brian Ború

His given name was Brian mac Cennétig. He was born into a minor family that lived in what is now south-east Co. Clare, near the Viking port of Limerick. The name by which we know him, Brian Ború, is an anglicized form of Brian Bóruma, from Béal Bóruma, a place name in his native territory. His family was part of an extended kinship network known collectively as Dál Cais, whose ultimate allegiance was to the kings of Munster. In 976, Brian's brother Mathgamain was murdered and Brian succeeded to the kingship of Dál Cais. He quickly consolidated his authority in Munster, displaying exceptional military ability and political cunning.

Within two years, he was King of Munster. The existing dynasty, the Eoghanachta, had been the principal power in the province for centuries. But internal divisions in what was – like all Gaelic warlord societies – a coalition of interlocking tribal dependencies gave Brian his opportunity. He seized it. With his power in Munster now established, he pressed on the marginal lordships and sub-kingdoms of Leinster. Bit by bit, he absorbed territories in Leinster during the 980s and 990s until he was checked by his near contemporary Mael Sechnaill II (Malachy), the king of the southern branch of the great Uí Néill (O'Neill) dynasty based at Tara, Co. Meath.

In 997, Brian and Mael Sechnaill concluded a truce, leaving Brian the most powerful figure in the southern half of the island. The two warlords' armies even coalesced to defeat the Vikings of Dublin in battle in 999. Three years later, the truce between Brian and Mael Sechnaill broke down. Mael Sechnaill, who had been the principal obstacle to Brian's further ambitions, was deposed. The way north was now clearer.

By 1005, he had achieved what few thought possible – he had gained effective control of the whole island by securing the submission of all the Uí Néill, both the southern and northern branches. He supported the claims of the diocese of Armagh to primacy in the Irish Church, on the grounds that St Patrick had chosen it as his principal church. This was a strange decision for a king from distant Munster to make but Brian knew the value of a key ecclesiastical ally, especially one based in potentially hostile territory. He made a gift of twenty ounces of gold to the clergy of Armagh. It was in the Book of Armagh that he was awarded the title *imperator Scottorum*, or Emperor of the Irish.

By now, Brian had come closer than anyone before or since to claiming the high kingship of Ireland. Such claims had been made in the past, especially by the Uí Néill, but such power as this gave them came from the ability to compel provincial kings to obedience through intermediaries rather than by military conquest. That is where Brian was different. He had imposed himself militarily on the entire island, the most successful warlord of them all.

But a warlord society was not the same as a royal kingdom. There was no Lord's anointed, endorsed by the Pope, at its head. There was no central authority with revenue-raising powers and a unique control of the military. Rather, it had some of the characteristics of a Mafia society, where power depended on main force and the charisma (and potential malevolence) of a strong leader. Brian's power was resented and, in 1013, the Leinster kingdoms revolted against his rule, leading to the Battle of Clontarf, on the north shore of Dublin Bay, in 1014. Viking mercenaries were engaged on both sides. The battle was later represented in nationalist myth as a war of liberation in which Gaelic Ireland conquered the Viking invaders. It was no such thing.

It was, instead, an attempt by the Leinster kings to recover what they had lost: provincial autonomy. They failed, but Brian's victory was, as noted above, a Pyrrhic one. He was killed, as were his son and young grandson. The Munster men's victory robbed them of their king (and his successors) and so weakened them that they could no longer aspire to that assertion of insular sovereignty which had been the essence of Brian's claim to the high kingship.

Brian Ború had done what nobody had done before and what no one would do again in Gaelic Ireland. After his death, despite fitful attempts by the Uí Néill to claim the high kingship, no strong political centre was established. Instead, the old pattern resumed. The O'Briens, as Brian Ború's successors now called themselves, fought for supremacy with the Uí Néill, although by the middle of the twelfth century both had to yield to the rising power of the O'Connors of Connacht. Their claim to the high kingship was to prove little more than rhetorical, as events would soon prove.

For the Irish world was about to be turned upside down.

Strongbow

Richard fitz Gilbert, also known as Richard de Clare and known most commonly as Strongbow, was not the first Norman invader of Ireland. But he was the most potent. He arrived at the invitation of Diarmait Mac Murchada, the deposed King of Leinster, who solicited Norman arms in order to recover his kingdom. He was promised the hand of Diarmait's daughter Aoife and also succession to the lordship of Leinster. This was in complete defiance of Gaelic succession law.

In August 1170, Strongbow landed in the south-east with an army of about 600 men. A combination of cavalry and archers made this a formidable military force. Waterford fell to Strongbow and, shortly after, Dublin followed. Mac Murchada died in 1171 and Strongbow duly succeeded him.

Strongbow had previously been Earl of Pembroke but when Henry II had become King of England in 1154, he had dispossessed de Clare of that title. Relations between the two men were soured as a result and Henry now looked with alarm on the possibility that a semi-independent Norman kingdom might be established in Ireland. In the autumn of 1171, the king brought an army across, intending to secure Strongbow's acknowledgement of Henry's royal authority in the conquered lands.

He succeeded, thus beginning the involvement of the English crown with Ireland. The island was declared a lordship owing allegiance to Henry. The king even secured the formal submission of Rory O'Connor, the King of Connacht and the most powerful lord in Gaelic Ireland. However, this submission did not hold, and military difficulties on the margins of the expanding Norman lordships were to prove a persistent pattern for most of the medieval period.

For all that, the arrival of Strongbow and the Normans was utterly transformative. New patterns of land holding, the building of massive stone castles, the further development and expansion of towns and a new social order were the most visible manifestations of the new order. If the Norman settlement was incomplete – there was to be no complete English conquest of Ireland for another 500 years – it was also indelible.

Strongbow did not enjoy his new lordship for long. He died in 1176 and is buried in Christ Church Cathedral in Dublin. His tomb is one of the sights of the modern cathedral. With Aoife, he had had a son, Gilbert, who succeeded to the lordship but died young in the 1180s, and a daughter, Isabella. In 1189, she married William Marshall, who thereby became Lord of Leinster and eventually managed to recover Strongbow's lost earldom of Pembroke.

Hugh O'Neill

The Uí Néill/O'Neill dynasty had been the lords of central Ulster for the best part of a millennium when Hugh O'Neill – the last of the line – was born around 1550. His father Matthew was Baron of Dungannon under English law but his right to that title was contested. Matthew was murdered in 1558. His sons, Brian and Hugh, were fostered by a New English family near Dublin on the orders of the Lord Justice of Ireland, Henry Sidney. Brian was murdered in 1562 and by the time Hugh attained his majority and returned to Ulster he succeeded as Baron of Dungannon.

There were two parallel systems of lordship in Ulster. Under Gaelic law, The O'Neill was the chief of his people by ancient right. Under English law, he was Earl of Tyrone. In the late 1560s and

1570s, these titles were held by Turlough Luineach O'Neill. But as his power declined from the mid-1580s, Hugh was acknowledged as Earl of Tyrone by the House of Lords. Eventually, Turlough Luineach died in 1595 and Hugh now claimed the ancient title of The O'Neill. This was forbidden under English law but the Dublin administration turned a blind eye. By now, Hugh O'Neill was too powerful to confront.

In the meantime, continued New English pressure on the Gaelic lordships in the Ulster marchlands had finally tripped off the revolt known as the Nine Years' War. At first O'Neill, serpentine, cunning and unscrupulous, had affected continued loyalty to the crown. It was a deception that could not last. By 1595, O'Neill was in open revolt. He won a convincing military victory at Clontibret, routing an English army under Marshal Bagenal which had been riding to the relief of the town of Monaghan, then under siege from the rebels.

O'Neill proved the most able military commander in late Gaelic Ireland. A series of ceasefires and parleys did not last and when the conflict resumed he won a crushing victory at the Battle of the Yellow Ford in 1598. Bagenal lost his life. No English army had ever before suffered such a defeat in Ireland. But it had been a defensive ambush battle and, for whatever reason, O'Neill did not follow up this victory. It may be that he felt he lacked the resources for open warfare. But despite his hesitation, the English administration was now thoroughly frightened of him. The entire English conquest was threatened.

Although the English were by now utterly sick of the Irish war, Elizabeth I felt obliged to send over her favourite, the Earl of Essex, with a large army to confront O'Neill. His mission failed and he was replaced in 1600 by Charles Blount, Lord Mountjoy. In the meantime, O'Neill and his principal ally, Hugh O'Donnell of Tyrconnell (Donegal) had persuaded Spain to send a supporting force. With less success, they tried to broaden their national position by appealing to the Old English in The Pale – a small region centred on Dublin which was the only part of Ireland where direct English rule was effective – on the basis of Catholic solidarity. But the Old

English were solidly loyal to the crown: the time for a confessional appeal to faith and fatherland was not yet.

The Spaniards arrived in late 1601 – but they landed at Kinsale, Co. Cork, at the other end of the country from O'Neill's Ulster heartland. Mountjoy laid siege to the Spanish position. O'Neill marched his own troops into north Leinster, augmented his army with men raised there and marched south, making rendezvous with O'Donnell's forces. The combined army outnumbered Mountjoy by a factor of about three to one and they surrounded his position: the besiegers were now themselves besieged.

It was Christmas Eve. Both O'Neill and O'Donnell were reluctant to engage in open battle with the English, but the Spanish position was desperate and invited relief. Mountjoy, trapped between the two, sallied out against the Irish and won a decisive victory despite his lack of numbers. Perhaps O'Neill's caution about open warfare after the Yellow Ford had not been misplaced, after all.

Kinsale effectively ended the war. In 1602, Mountjoy was at last able to invade central Ulster, destroying the ancient inauguration stone of the O'Neills. In the following year, Hugh O'Neill finally submitted to the crown in a treaty signed at Mellifont, a ruined Cistercian abbey near Drogheda. He received reasonably generous terms and was able to resume his position in Ulster. But the Dublin administration maintained relentless pressure on the Gaelic lords of Ulster and in 1607, O'Neill, O'Donnell and others of the native aristocracy departed for the continent in the event known as the Flight of the Earls.

They intended to return but they never did. It was the end of Gaelic Ireland. The earls' lands were deemed forfeit to the crown and settled by new English and Scottish owners, a process known to history as the Plantation of Ulster. O'Neill had lost – but it had been a very close-run thing. England had come closer to outright defeat in Ireland than ever before or since.

Oliver Cromwell

If Hugh O'Neill was regarded as a hero, Cromwell was very definitely not. For, as the hallowed phrase has it, 'Cromwell like a lightning passed through the land'. He spent just ten months in Ireland but in that short time he set in process the final, absolute conquest of Ireland by English power.

The 1640s had been a chaotic decade in both islands. An Ulster Gaelic revolt in 1641 soon ran out of control and resulted in the slaughter of many Protestants, beneficiaries of the ongoing Plantation of Ulster. Two civil wars in England between parliament and the king culminated in victory for the former and execution for the latter, following which a republic was established under Cromwell's leadership. All this impacted on Ireland, which was inevitably drawn into the maelstrom. Cromwell arrived in Dublin in August 1649, just six months after the execution of Charles I, with an army of 12,000 men battle hardened in the English wars, supplemented by 8,000 troops already in Ireland who were loyal to the parliamentary cause. Critically, he also brought with him an advanced artillery train with men skilled in siege warfare.

It soon proved its worth. Cromwell marched north to lay siege to the town of Drogheda, near the mouth of the River Boyne. An earlier siege of the town, in 1642, had lasted for seven months. This one, thanks to the artillery, was over in a few days. Cromwell ordered the massacre of most of the officers of the garrison and the banishment of the men to Barbados as indentured servants – little better than slaves.

This single action shocked contemporary opinion and stained Cromwell's name in Irish nationalist memory for ever. He justified it as exemplary revenge for the Ulster massacres of 1641: 'I am persuaded that this is a righteous judgment of God upon these barbarous wretches who have imbrued their hands in so much innocent blood; and that it will tend to prevent the effusion of blood for the future.' The matter remains a source of historical dispute and debate to this day.

Cromwell was right about one thing, though. The massacre at Drogheda did 'prevent the effusion of blood for the future'. Other besieged towns in his path had no wish to share the fate of Drogheda and most submitted to him meekly. The only further resistance of any sort came from the town of Clonmel, Co. Tipperary and even that did not last long. By May 1650, most of Ireland was under Cromwellian control and he felt able to depart the island to attend to problems in Scotland.

He left behind a mopping-up operation which dragged on until 1652 when even the remote island of Inishbofin, off the coast of Co. Galway, was in English hands. At last the English were the undisputed masters of the entire island of Ireland. What followed was a massive plantation scheme. Cromwell dispossessed every Catholic landowner in the rich provinces of Munster and Leinster and replaced them with reliable English Protestants, who became the antecedents of the eighteenth-century ascendancy. The dispossessed were to remove to the poorer western province of Connacht.

This dispossession was done without any regard to the remote ethnic origins of the displaced Catholics. Old English and Gaelic lords alike, Cromwell saw only as an undifferentiated mass of Catholics, all of them complicit, more or less, in the Ulster horrors of 1641. The Cromwellian land confiscations set the pattern of Irish history for the next 250 years. It is no accident that when Irish nationalism eventually formed, it did so on the basis of Catholic solidarity. Cromwell had left a telling legacy.

Theobald Wolfe Tone

The epithet most commonly applied to Tone is 'father of Irish republicanism', which is fair enough. No one before him had framed a demand for republican separatism with such rhetorical clarity. He was the son of Peter Tone, a coachmaker who lived on the estate of the Wolfe family about fifteen miles south-west of Dublin. He was named for the young squire Theobald Wolfe.

From an early age, Tone displayed a giddy intelligence. His earliest ambition was to become a soldier and all his life he was attracted to the military. However, at his father's insistence he entered Trinity College Dublin to study law. He made a mark on college life. He won medals for oratory in the Historical Society, one of Trinity's two principal debating societies, and was elected auditor in his final year. He was not the most diligent student and even took a year out, which he spent engrossed in military books, still hankering for a soldier's life. However, he eventually graduated in 1786. He was 23.

Tone had charm in abundance and a gift for friendship, something that he retained until the end. He also had a wife, for he had eloped with and married a 15-year-old, Matilda Witherington. The circumstances of his marriage did not exactly endear him to the Witheringtons. Moreover, it meant that he could not pursue a fellowship in Trinity. He resolved on the law, left his new wife in the care of her family and took himself off to the Middle Temple in London, from which he emerged as a barrister in the fateful year of 1789.

He returned to Dublin and practised law for a while, although it bored him. He was much more drawn to politics; the excited temper of the times, in the heady early days of the French Revolution, raised liberal and radical hopes everywhere. Tone became known as a trenchant pamphleteer and gradually he moved from conventional Whig liberalism to a more forthright republicanism. The 'tree of liberty' was being planted in Irish soil.

Nowhere was this truer than in Belfast, the principal town – it was scarcely a city at this time – of Ulster. Its Presbyterian population suffered disadvantages at the hands of the Anglican elite, not as severe as those endured by Roman Catholics but vexing none the less. Moreover, the democratic impulse in Presbyterian church government – its non-hierarchical and levelling tendencies – made the principles of the early French Revolution attractive. Tone became friendly with one Thomas Russell, originally from Cork, a half-pay army officer who, after service in India, had been stationed in Belfast.

Russell, known ever after as 'The Man from God Knows Where', had been influenced by the republican spirit of Presbyterian Belfast. He asked Tone to draft some resolutions which could be put to a meeting of the Volunteers – a reforming militia – on the second anniversary of the fall of the Bastille. Crucially, it included a proposal that Roman Catholics be fully admitted to Irish public life. This was an issue that bedevilled all Whiggish reform movements of the 1780s, and so it proved again. This resolution was suppressed.

Angered, Tone responded by writing a pamphlet entitled 'An Argument on Behalf of the Catholics of Ireland'. It was a sensation, putting the case for equality with clarity and force. He was invited to Belfast where he renewed his friendship with Russell. In October 1791, they were among the founder members of the Society of United Irishmen. The following month the Dublin branch of the United Irishmen was formed.

Despite its calls for full equality for Catholics, there were residual doubts on every side. Some Presbyterian radicals doubted if the members of what they regarded as an authoritarian church were fit for liberty. Catholics, in their turn, were suspicious of Presbyterians. This division of sentiment was echoed in other developments during the 1790s. Were the United Irishmen a radical reforming or a revolutionary separatist organization? This became an urgent question when Britain entered the revolutionary wars against France in 1794. The two countries were to be at war for most of the following twenty-one years.

In the meantime, in 1792, Tone had been appointed assistant secretary to the Catholic Committee in Dublin, whose radical element had been impressed by his advocacy. He proved an energetic agent, organizing a convention of Catholics from all parts of Ireland in Dublin in late 1792 which adopted a resolution in favour of Catholic rights. Moreover, Tone then accompanied a delegation to London where the resolution was presented to King George III.

The growing tensions with France persuaded the British government to appease Irish Catholics and a modest measure of reform was passed in 1793. The Catholic Committee dissolved itself, considering its work a success. Tone did not, regarding the Relief Act as a sop. When war did break out, the government cracked down on radicals everywhere. A French spy in Dublin was arrested; he had had some dealings with Tone, who found himself compromised. He did a deal with the authorities, whereby he confirmed information they already had in return for his freedom. He resolved to go to America.

By 1795, he was settled in Philadelphia but early the following year he made his way to France to solicit assistance of the Directory in an invasion of Ireland. He found himself pushing an open door, as the French had been contemplating such a step themselves. The upshot was the arrival of three ships and about 15,000 crack French troops in Bantry Bay, in the south-west of Ireland, in December 1796. But contrary winds frustrated them; they were unable to land – to the immense frustration of Tone – and the invasion force returned to France.

Tone played no direct part in the Rising of 1798 but he was part of a feeble French supporting invasion, which was all too little and too late. In the uniform of a French officer, he landed in Co. Donegal in late October, long after the main rebellion had been suppressed. He was recognized, taken to Dublin, charged with treason, and committed suicide while under sentence of death.

Tone's non-sectarian republican idealism introduced a redemptive strain into Irish nationalism, which otherwise tended to coalesce around Catholic solidarity. His legacy was to be recognized as the posthumous keeper of the Irish nationalist conscience.

Daniel O'Connell

If Tone was resolutely anti-sectarian, the same could hardly be said of Daniel O'Connell. The failure of the 1798 rebellion had polarized religious opinion in Ireland. Protestants of all sorts who had previously held liberal opinions generally abandoned them, thoroughly frightened by the open sectarianism of some incidents, especially in Co. Wexford, during that tragic summer. The Act of Union of 1801 abolished the semi-independent Irish parliament, while Protestant ultras cracked the whip in the Dublin Castle administration.

This was the world in which O'Connell came to maturity. The son of an old Catholic gentry family from a remote part of Co. Kerry, he had been educated in France, at Douai, and on returning to Ireland he became a barrister. He was one of the first generation of Catholics allowed to practise law under the terms of the 1793 Catholic Relief Act. In due time, he would become the most famous advocate in Ireland.

From the early years of the nineteenth century and still in his twenties, he involved himself in the twin causes that defined his life and career: Catholic Emancipation and repeal of the Act of Union. From 1808 on, he made his name by his opposition to any measure of Catholic relief that might entail the British government having a veto over Catholic episcopal appointments. This early assertion of Catholic independence split Catholic opinion but gradually the anti-veto element proved to be the majority.

The controversy impelled reformers in a more radical and more assertively Catholic direction. In 1823, O'Connell founded the Catholic Association. Similar associations had been launched on and off without success since the height of the veto controversy in the previous decade. What made the difference this time was the so-called Catholic Rent, a subscription of a penny a month which almost immediately created a mass movement by admitting labourers and peasants to a world previously reserved for the well-to-do.

This was the first populist, mass mobilization of an entire people in European history. The government suppressed it, only for it to be reborn under a different name. The Association created a national network of local committees and activists by tapping into the one existing organizational structure that was tailor-made for the purpose: the Catholic parish system.

There was a general election in 1826. Although Catholics were not permitted to sit in parliament, many liberal Protestants stood in support of the Catholic cause. The key contest was in Co. Waterford, where the Tory candidate was Lord George Thomas Beresford, son of the powerful Marquis of Waterford. His liberal opponent was one Villiers Stuart, who won. Waterford's tenants had abandoned him, transferring their allegiance to the candidate supported by the Catholic Association – risking eviction or other sanctions as a result.

There followed the tumultuous 1828 by-election in Co. Clare in which O'Connell, although barred because of his religion from taking his seat if successful, stood against Vesey Fitzgerald. Ironically, Fitzgerald was a liberal supporter of Emancipation but O'Connell none the less traduced him with the most uncompromising sectarian rhetoric. His appeal was directly to Catholic grievances, to the embittered collective memory of dispossession, discrimination and humiliation. Every parish priest in the county bar one worked on O'Connell's campaign.

He won. The Tory government in London, jointly led by the Duke of Wellington and Sir Robert Peel, were now in a bind, fearing outright electoral revolt in Ireland – and the threat of worse. In the end, and with a bad grace, they conceded. Catholic Emancipation was passed in 1829 and O'Connell, at 54 years of age, was the man of the hour.

To his contemporaries, he was a mixture of hero and enigma. He had titanic energy and organizing ability; a sulphurous temper; torrential eloquence; vast reservoirs of charm. He was a genuine liberal in many respects, as his parliamentary career was to prove: a free trader, an anti-slaver, a philosemite. Yet he led a movement that was nakedly confessional. He stands accused of introducing the priest into Irish politics. He might have replied that he could only work with the tools to hand.

He achieved a number of reforms in the 1830s, working in co-operation with Whig governments. In particular, he helped to broker a settlement of the much-resented tithe question, whereby Catholics were obliged to contribute to the upkeep of the Anglican Church of Ireland. But the big question now was Repeal of the Union.

The Tories returned to power under Peel in 1841. O'Connell formed the Repeal Association along lines similar to the old Catholic Association. A series of so-called Monster Meetings were intended to intimidate the government by sheer weight of numbers. But Peel – an old adversary of O'Connell – stood firm. Two other factors told against the movement. It did not have anything like the same degree of clerical support as Emancipation had had: it was a national, rather than a specifically Catholic, cause. Critically, the Repeal movement failed completely in Protestant Ulster – a portent for the future.

The Repeal agitation peaked in 1843 when O'Connell, fearing violence, cancelled a Monster Meeting scheduled for Clontarf in north Dublin. He was convicted of conspiracy anyway and spent the summer of 1844 in comfortable confinement in jail. In the eyes of his younger and more radical supporters, his climb-down at Clontarf was an act of cowardice. They advocated a more assertive policy, not excluding violence. Although O'Connell retained substantial majority support, he was failing. Ireland was overwhelmed by the catastrophe of the Great Famine.

O'Connell set out for a final journey to Rome but died at Genoa in January 1847. He had brought into being the mainstream tradition of Irish nationalism, both its benign and its ugly sides. It was an impressive achievement and Ireland still lives with the legacy he left it.

Charles Stewart Parnell

The Parnell family originated in Cheshire. Thomas Parnell, whose uncle and grandfather had each been mayor of Congleton, was a beneficiary of the Cromwellian plantation. He secured an estate in Queen's County (Laois) and settled down to life as a country gentleman. That was in the 1660s.

A number of descendants distinguished themselves, but the first to make an impact on Irish public life was Sir John Parnell, who rose to be Chancellor of the Irish Exchequer in the late eighteenth century. He was a principled opponent of the Act of Union, a fact that did no harm to his great-grandson's political prospects. One of his sons, William Parnell, inherited the house and estate at Avondale, Co. Wicklow, in 1795, where Charles Stewart Parnell was born in 1846.

Parnell's mother was an American, Delia Stewart, the daughter of Admiral Stewart – Old Ironsides – who had distinguished himself in the American war against the British in 1812. Her father's dislike of the British rubbed off on her and her dislike in turn rubbed off on her son. None the less, he was reared in the conventional manner of an Irish country gentleman, being schooled in England and then going on to Cambridge, from which he was expelled *sans* degree.

On 1 September 1870 the Home Government Association was launched in Dublin by Isaac Butt, a barrister and former MP. Irish nationalism and the cause of Repeal had been in the doldrums since the twin disasters of O'Connell's death and the Great Famine of 1845–52. Butt's movement aspired to a vague compromising of the Act of Union to allow for some degree of autonomy or devolution. The term deployed was wonderfully vague and elastic: home rule.

In time, as the 1870s wore on, home rule came to assume a more obviously nationalist colour. It attracted the allegiance of out-and-out nationalists in growing numbers. At the 1874 general election that brought Disraeli to power in London, the home rulers took 59 Irish seats. Butt was a decent man, but no leader. He was rather too gentlemanly and deferential for the Westminster bear pit.

Enter Parnell. He was elected for Co. Meath in a by-election in 1875 and within a few years he had displaced Butt as party leader. Moreover, he had made friends among the Fenians – a revolutionary, republican group which represented the radical edge of Irish nationalism – and persuaded them to back a policy of co-operation. Hitherto, the Fenians had been disdainful of parliamentary politics. Now they committed to working with Parnell.

This led to the formation of the Land League, which pressed for land reform and tenant rights. Land agitation and parliamentary disruption now marched hand in hand and convulsed Ireland in the early 1880s. The campaign succeeded: a series of land reforms were effected which gradually unstitched the Cromwellian land settlement, first by weakening the absolute property rights of landlords and later by buying out their interests entirely and establishing the former tenants as owner-occupiers. The whole process took more than twenty years to come to fulfilment.

In the meantime, Parnell had established iron control and discipline over his parliamentary party at Westminster and in the Irish constituencies. The core demand moved gradually from the land question to a more assertive claim for home rule; that is, for the restoration of a parliament in Dublin to deal with domestic Irish affairs. A series of indecisive general elections in the mid-1880s left Parnell's party holding the balance of power at Westminster. This prompted Gladstone, the Liberal Party leader, to support Irish home rule in return for Parnell's support.

The 1886 Home Rule bill split the Liberals and was defeated. But in Ireland, it seemed not like the end of a process but the beginning. Parnell had achieved a miracle: one of the two great British parties – indeed, the one that had been in power more often than not since the 1840s – was now committed to home rule for Ireland. Surely the pendulum of parliamentary politics would deliver the goods in time. What had been unthinkable a few years earlier had become one of the central questions in British public life. Parnell was a god in Ireland.

And, like a god, he fell. When his affair with Katharine O'Shea, wife of one of his most useless MPs, was discovered he was disowned by Gladstone's Liberals. The party, with its strong roots in dissenting Protestantism, was prone to fits of moral panic. The Nonconformist Conscience was dusted down and aired. Gladstone was now faced with either sacrificing Parnell or losing the leadership of the Liberals. He presented the Nationalist Party with a hideous dilemma: it could have Parnell or the Liberal alliance but not both.

The party split on 15 December 1890. The majority chose the Liberals. Parnell attempted to reconstruct his political fortunes in a series of three bitterly fought by-election campaigns over the following year, all of which he lost. The Irish Catholic hierarchy, hitherto staunch supporters, turned against Parnell the adulterer, determined not to be out-moralized by a crowd of English Protestants. The split was a savage business, the venom of which has never been better rendered than in the Christmas dinner scene in Joyce's *A Portrait of the Artist as a Young Man*. Passions were inflamed beyond reason on both sides. It darkened Irish nationalist life for a generation.

Parnell's frenzied by-election campaigns killed him. Never robust, he was drenched to the skin while addressing a meeting in Creggs, Co. Roscommon and caught a chill which developed into pneumonia. He dragged himself back to Katharine in England and died there on 6 October 1891. His remains were returned to Dublin, where his funeral attracted over 100,000 mourners. He is buried in the most impressive grave in Ireland, in Glasnevin cemetery under a single granite boulder from his native county of Wicklow, bearing the simple legend PARNELL.

W.B. Yeats

Yeats was born in the prosperous Dublin suburb of Sandymount in June 1865. His father, John B. Yeats, was a young barrister, for whom a glittering career at the Bar was predicted. He had also inherited a country estate and another town house from his father, who had been a clergyman. His mother likewise came of solid bourgeois stock: Susan Yeats, née Pollexfen, was the daughter of a wealthy Sligo shipping family. The poet, who was later to affect aristocratic airs, was in fact born into the middle class.

John Yeats soon wearied of the law and set up instead as a portrait painter, for which he had a genuine talent but which lowered his standing socially. The family moved to London and paid a heavy price materially for Yeats *père*'s change of career. In 1872, when young Willie was seven, they were obliged to fall back on the Pollexfens in Sligo, going there on what began as a holiday but lasted for more than two years. It was a crucial moment in the formation of the future poet.

The boy fell in love with the place: the landscape, the folklore, fairy stories related by servants. These stories, augmented by the nautical adventures and tall tales which are the staple of any shipping household, gave him a fascination with the irrational that never left him. One key to understanding Yeats is his attraction to magic and his recoil from the world of mere empirical reality. From now on, Sligo was firmly imprinted on his consciousness, even after the family returned to London.

He was first educated at home by his father and then at the Godolphin School in Hammersmith. He was a mediocre student, displaying no precocious talents. What really animated him was not the formal world of education but the artistic milieu in which his father moved. The primacy of the arts was an idea planted early in his mind. It never left him.

His first substantial volume of poetry, *The Wanderings of Oisin and Other Poems*, appeared in 1889, when Willie was 24. It was in a tradition of Anglo-Irish verse – poetry on Irish themes written in English – which had been developing throughout the nineteenth century. Often thought of as the fountainhead of a poetic tradition, Yeats was equally the inheritor of one that had already produced some distinguished work. This first volume was also influenced by the medieval romanticism of William Morris and by Yeats' involvement with the Theosophical Society, an esoteric and occult movement founded by a remarkable Russian woman, Madame Blavatsky.

Morris and Blavatsky hint at another important feature of Yeats' life, and one that is easily overlooked. His association with Ireland is so strong that it is easy to forget that he spent nearly half his life in England, mostly in London. In 1890, he deepened his association with magic and the irrational by joining the Order of the Golden Dawn, having been expelled from Blavatsky's group for holding heterodox opinions.

During the 1890s, he published a novel, an influential collection of short stories, two volumes of poetry and a number of plays. The plays planted the seed of a national Irish dramatic movement which would come to fruition in the foundation of the Abbey Theatre in 1904. His love for Maud Gonne, whom he first met in 1889, drew him into Irish nationalist circles and he may even have been inducted into the Fenians. But although Yeats was to have a notable career as a public man, art always came first. It may account for the fact that his love for Maud Gonne was not reciprocated. For her, it was the other way round.

For her, however, Yeats wrote his most incendiary political play, *The Countess Cathleen* (1899). Gonne played the eponymous heroine in a work that was a barely disguised call to arms. Its provocations troubled the poet's conscience in later years. The early years of the Abbey were dominated by the works of John Millington Synge, whose *The Playboy of the Western World* offended nationalist pieties. Once again, Yeats' passionate defence of it was grounded in the assertion that art owed no duty to politics.

In 1909, he met Ezra Pound for the first time. Under his influence, Yeats' work adopts a more modern rhetoric and register, as he began to shed the Pre-Raphaelite sensibility that had sustained him until now. The collection *Responsibilities* (1914) marks the change, both in theme and diction. The spirit world of magic is replaced by a poetry of public engagement, most famously in 'Easter 1916', his superb response to the Easter Rising, which, although dated September 1916, was first published only in a private limited edition in the following year and not in book form until 1921.

The greatest sustained period of his poetic life now began. The Irish War of Independence (1919–21) and especially the civil war that followed the Treaty settlement with Britain (1922–23) prompted some of his very finest work. 'Meditations in Time of Civil War', a seven-part tour de force, and 'Nineteen Hundred and Nineteen' are but two examples. Nor was it just Ireland: a whole world had collapsed in the Great War and Yeats wrote some of his most brilliant and most frequently quoted lines in 'The Second Coming':

> Turning and turning in the widening gyre
> The falcon cannot hear the falconer;

Things fall apart; the centre cannot hold;
   Mere anarchy is loosed upon the world,
...
The best lack all conviction, while the worst
Are full of passionate intensity
...
And what rough beast, its hour come round at last,
Slouches towards Bethlehem to be born?

This sense of abandonment in a world changed disastrously for the worse also informs poems such as 'A Prayer for my Daughter'. The onset of old age prompted what many consider his masterpiece, 'Sailing to Byzantium'. As he aged in the 1930s, he flirted with fascism – foolishly seeing it as an aristocratic bulwark against Bolshevism. He was not alone in his foolishness. He had finally married an Englishwoman, Georgina Hyde-Lees, in 1917 but now, aware of failing sexual powers, embarked on a number of affairs with younger women.

Yeats died in France in 1939 and his body was returned to Ireland after World War II. He was a poet of immense power and reach; in the opinion of many the finest English-language poet of the twentieth century. He had won the Nobel Prize for Literature in 1923 but it is for the great poems of his maturity, from 1914 onwards, that he will be celebrated for as long as English literature lives.

James Joyce

Joyce was born in Dublin in 1882 and died in Zurich in 1941. In some respects, one could leave it at that because, unlike Yeats, Joyce was never a public figure. His thoughts and opinions on public affairs were only occasionally articulated and were of little account in the greater scheme of his life. That life was about one thing and one thing only: literature.

He produced four major works, three of them masterpieces. For all that I know, the fourth, *Finnegans Wake*, may be as well, but like many others I find it too impenetrable: much as I want to give JJ the benefit of the doubt on the *Wake*, it leaves me lost and bewildered. As for the other three, however, there is no doubt.

Dubliners, his breakthrough book, is by common consent the finest collection of short stories in the language; the last story, 'The Dead', is the supreme achievement of short-form fiction. A *Portrait of the Artist as a Young Man* is an autobiographical *Bildungsroman* of exceptional grace and power, tracing the young Joyce's development from childhood to young adult and culminating in the moment that he resolves to leave Ireland.

Both are written with a clarity almost amounting to simplicity. The writing is utterly transparent and presents no unusual challenge to the reader. The same cannot be said for the third masterpiece, Joyce's wonder-novel, *Ulysses*. It is, in my view, the greatest novel ever written but it can be opaque, obscure, maddeningly self-indulgent, boring in places. Still, there is nothing like it and if it requires a few early efforts to get into it, as it did with me and many others, the rewards are beyond wonderful. For all its faults, this is the funniest book ever written – a great comic affirmation of human life.

Ulysses is many things, a vast arabesque of a book; a celebration of the ordinary and the everyday; a chronicle of urban life which it captures with uncanny fidelity. No city – not even Dickens' London – has come alive on the page in the way that Dublin does in Joyce's great book. Moreover, it is wrong to over-emphasize the obscurities of style, because most of the book is perfectly accessible to any literate adult.

The narrative is simple enough. Stephen Dedalus, the brilliant young intellectual, has left his father's house and is lodging with some student acquaintances. In the course of the day – the entire action is contained in less than twenty-four hours – he has breakfast, teaches in a school, wanders on the beach, has a discussion about Hamlet with savants in the National Library, goes drinking with medical students and ends up in a brothel.

In the meantime, Leopold Bloom, an advertising salesman, starts his day in his house in Eccles Street. He makes breakfast for his wife Molly, goes about his business (which is conducted at a leisurely pace) in the course of which he meets many people he knows in a city where everyone is known, attends a funeral, has lunch, pops into the National Library at the same time that Stephen is there but does not meet him, briefly visits a pub where he is abused by a nationalist fanatic and eventually rescues Stephen from a brawl with soldiers in the brothel quarter.

This is the climactic moment of the book, the meeting of spiritual father and spiritual son. What follows is really a long coda as they make their way back to Eccles Street where Bloom has offered Stephen shelter for the night. The book ends by switching back to Molly Bloom, already in bed – where she had earlier spent an adulterous afternoon with a character called Blazes Boylan – to record her half-awake, half-asleep monologue.

The plot is not the point. The story is told from a series of shifting and highly elaborated points of view, with a huge cast of minor characters. The celebrated series of internal monologues – more usually referred to as stream of consciousness – allows the reader inside the heads of the principal characters. The action criss-crosses the Edwardian city not just on the day in question – 16 June 1904 – but also recalls past events from the characters' lives, especially those of Bloom and Molly. In Molly's case, this takes us far away from Dublin to Gibraltar where her father, an army officer, had been stationed when she was a girl.

But Dublin is everywhere in the book, like a scent. The locales reach from Dalkey on the far south of the bay to Howth Head at the northern end and take in most of the city centre together with suburbs and nearby mountains in the recollections of various characters. Even with all the changes in the century since the book was set and written, the sense of authenticity – for anyone familiar with Dublin – is uncanny, a point that has been made repeatedly over the years.

Its physical descriptions, the fidelity with which Joyce captures the cadences and rhetoric of Dublin speech, its miraculous insinuation of the city's atmosphere on to the printed page are such that many people who have never been to Dublin first apprehend the city from *Ulysses* and then discover a familiar place when they eventually arrive in person.

Bloom is the hero of the book, like Homer's Ulysses a wanderer. He is Everyman – ordinary, disappointed, kindly, weak. There is nothing heroic about Bloom; rather, he is the quintessence of democratic man, the most fully realized modern character in fiction. We learn more about him, and about his thoughts, recollections, anxieties and doubts, than we do of any other fictional creation. He is literature's greatest Joe Soap.

Edward Carson

Hero or villain? It depends on where you are standing. For Irish nationalists, he was the evil genius who mobilized Ulster unionist resistance to home rule. For unionists, he was the charismatic genius who kept Protestant Ulster out of the Catholic-dominated home rule state to the south. For devotees of Oscar Wilde, he was the unpleasant barrister who destroyed their hero in the witness box in 1895.

Carson was a Dubliner, born in 1854. His father was a successful architect and builder. He was educated at Trinity College Dublin, where he was a contemporary of Oscar Wilde. Carson was a plodder whereas Wilde carried off every prize with dash and *élan*: this was to prove a fateful conjunction. He took a primary degree in classics and then read for the Bar. He qualified in 1877 and two years later he married.

His early career at the Bar was unspectacular. In the 1880s, however, the various land agitations were to prove the making of him. The young Arthur Balfour was appointed Chief Secretary of Ireland by his uncle, the Prime Minister Lord Salisbury. Balfour resolved on a policy of coercion and a strict application of the law against all forms of tenant unrest. This earned him the sobriquet 'Bloody Balfour' and in the various prosecutions by which this policy was carried forward Carson came to be the leading counsel for the crown.

He formed a close alliance with Balfour, whom he greatly admired. By the age of 35, he had taken silk and was the youngest QC in Ireland. In 1892, he was appointed solicitor-general for Ireland and was elected to the House of Commons as MP for Trinity College. His place in parliament took him to England; he abandoned his Irish practice and established himself in the Middle Temple.

It was the cross-examination of Oscar Wilde that made Carson's name in England. Wilde's lover was Lord Alfred Douglas, the son of the Marquess of Queensberry who left an insulting note for Wilde at his club. Wilde initiated a prosecution for criminal libel against Queensberry, for whom Carson acted in defence. His patient, plodding but devastating cross-examination destroyed Wilde. In 1900, he was appointed solicitor-general of England and was knighted.

All of this would have been nothing more than a conventional account of a successful professional career except for Ulster. In 1910, Carson became leader of the Irish Unionist Party at the moment when the prospect of home rule for Ireland – to which Unionists were implacably opposed – was firmly back on the British political agenda. It was one thing to oppose the threatened measure: it was quite another to mobilize opposition effectively.

That opposition was focused on Ulster, the only Irish region where Protestant and unionist numbers were concentrated. Sir James Craig was the local organizer of resistance but it was Carson who gave the anti-home-rule movement its voice and its rhetoric. His leadership of the campaign saw the signing of the Ulster Solemn League and Covenant; the mobilization of the paramilitary Ulster Volunteer Force; the illegal landing of arms for the UVF at Larne, Co. Antrim; and a patient, assiduous use of his British political connections to frustrate nationalist ambitions.

As a Dubliner, he hoped that Ulster resistance to home rule would save all of Ireland for the union. It was not to be. Partition, unthinkable only a few years earlier, became inevitable as the irresistible force of nationalism met the immovable object of regional unionism. Ireland was indeed partitioned. A regional parliament was established in Belfast under nominal supervision of Westminster. An ostentatious pile of a parliament house was built in solidly Protestant east Belfast at Stormont and in the grounds leading to there was erected a statue of Edward Carson, the father of Northern Ireland. It is still there.

Patrick Pearse

If Carson represented one pole of Irishness, Pearse represented the other. He was born in 1879, the son of an Irish mother and an English father. James Pearse was an ecclesiastical stone carver, a trade for which there was much demand in Ireland in the second half of the nineteenth century as the Catholic Church building boom persisted. Patrick was educated by the Christian Brothers, whose utilitarian, Gradgrind philosophy of education he came to loathe. When in later life he opened his own school, it was to espouse an educational philosophy remote from and vastly more enlightened than that of the Brothers.

They did, however, introduce the young Pearse to the Irish language. It was a transformative moment in his life. He joined the Gaelic League in 1896 as his schooldays were ending but before he went to university. The League had been established three years earlier with the aim of reviving Irish as the common vernacular of the country. Within two years of joining, Pearse had made a sufficient mark to be co-opted to its executive committee, bringing him into close contact with people influential in the wider Irish cultural revival of the time. He was not yet 20. He was already teaching Irish in his old school and now began to give classes in the Royal University, where he failed to impress his contemporary James Joyce, who thought him a bore.

Nominally, the Gaelic League was non-political. But its implied purpose was clear: the re-Gaelicization of Ireland. That was a purpose that could not be kept innocent of politics for ever; not in a country like Ireland. Its natural attraction was to a generation of young nationalists disillusioned with conventional politics following the fall of Parnell and looking for a cultural channel for their anglophobia.

By 1903, Pearse was editor of the Gaelic League newspaper, *An Claidheamh Soluis* (The Sword of Light). In 1908 he founded a bilingual secondary school, St Enda's, whose ethos was grounded in cultural nationalism. Indeed, Pearse's nationalism was very much of the cultural variety at this time, in common with that of many of his contemporaries. He supported home rule but without much passion or conviction.

As with so many others, it was the quickening events of the years after 1910 that radicalized him. The revival of physical-force nationalism in the face of unionist resistance to home rule saw the establishment of the Irish Volunteers in 1913. Pearse joined. But within the Volunteers, a key element was the Irish Republican Brotherhood – otherwise known as the Fenians – an uncompromising secret body devoted to revolutionary violence. And within the IRB, there was formed an even more secret cabal, the Military Council, which planned the Easter Rising of 1916.

Pearse was now in this inner revolutionary sanctum and when the Rising occurred, he was one of the seven signatories of the Proclamation of the Republic, which he read to a bemused crowd outside the GPO following its investment by the rebels. He was nominally commander-in-chief of the Volunteers and President of the Irish Republic proclaimed on that Easter Monday.

When the Rising was eventually suppressed the following Saturday, it was Pearse who made the formal surrender to the British. He was court-martialled, convicted and executed on 3 May 1916. Of all the leaders of the Rising, he was the one who became an icon. His image is still instantly recognizable and his oratory still frequently quoted – not least his magnificent eulogy delivered over the grave of the old Fenian Jeremiah O'Donovan Rossa in 1915.

Michael Collins

Collins was the Napoleonic force of nature in the Irish revolution. Dead before his 32nd birthday, he left an indelible mark on the country. A country boy from West Cork, while still in his teens he moved to London, where he worked first as a post office clerk and later for a firm of stockbrokers. He also became involved with the secret Irish Republican Brotherhood. Back in Ireland in 1915, he fought in the GPO during the Easter Rising the following year.

He was not one of the leaders of the Rising and there was never any question of his being executed. Instead, he was interned for a while in a remote part of Wales along with other rebels. On his release in 1917, he returned to Ireland and rapidly established a position of influence in the revived Sinn Féin party, which now became the principal voice of Irish nationalism in place of the old home rulers.

When Sinn Féin swept the board in Ireland in the December 1918 general election, it acted on party policy, refused to take its seats at Westminster and instead constituted itself as Dáil Éireann (the parliament of Ireland) in Dublin. It established a shadow administration, in which Collins was successively Minister for Home Affairs and Minister for Finance. In the latter role, he raised a Dáil loan of £350,000 – the target had been £100,000 – and which financed the alternative administration and its Dáil courts.

But Collins' real influence came from his position as Director of Organization and Intelligence of the IRA, as the Volunteers had now become. Moreover, he was President of the Supreme Council of the IRB, giving him a key role at the secret heart of revolutionary conspiracy. He directed military policy in the War of Independence, targeting the police – the Royal Irish Constabulary – in remote and exposed country barracks. By forcing their withdrawal in many places, he deprived the Dublin Castle administration of vital sources of local information.

In the meantime, he created his own formidable intelligence

operation, with spies in the heart of the British administration reporting to him. He evoked huge personal loyalty from his colleagues – and, it may be said, jealousy and dislike from some that he crossed. He had a personal staff known as the Squad and it was they who assassinated fourteen British intelligence officers on the morning of 21 November 1920, provoking a British reprisal that afternoon when a party of Auxiliaries – an armed police reserve force – fired on the crowd at a Gaelic Football match at Croke Park, killing twelve spectators and a player and injuring over sixty.

By the middle of 1921, it was clear that some form of negotiation was required to resolve the situation in Ireland. The leader of Sinn Féin, Éamon de Valera, who had been in the United States on a fund-raising and propaganda mission for eighteen months, had returned to Ireland. He concluded a truce with the British Prime Minster, David Lloyd George, in July. In October, a delegation of five members of the Dáil was dispatched to London to negotiate a Treaty of Settlement with the British.

Fatefully, de Valera was not one of the delegation but Collins was. It was a decision that has continued to mystify people. De Valera was the most sinuous and serpentine negotiator available to Sinn Féin, yet he absented himself. Collins, the man of action who had come to personify the war in Ireland, felt that the negotiating table was not his natural milieu. None the less, he was a party to a treaty secured on 6 December but immediately disowned by de Valera and his associates because it fell short of the full republican demand.

The Dáil approved the treaty by a narrow margin. De Valera withdrew and Collins became chairman of the Provisional Government that was now formed. A civil war ensued, lasting from June 1922 until April 1923, which resulted in victory for the pro-treaty side, which proceeded to establish the Irish Free State. By then Collins was dead, killed by a sniper's bullet in his own county of Cork in August 1922.

Some idea of the effect Collins had on his contemporaries may be gathered from the note of condolence that George Bernard Shaw wrote to Hannie Collins, his sister:

Dear Miss Collins, Don't let them make you miserable about it: how could a born soldier die better than at the victorious end of a good fight, falling to the shot of another Irishman – a damned fool, but all the same an Irishman who thought he was fighting for Ireland – a 'Roman to Roman'? I met Michael for the first and last time on Saturday last, and am very glad I did. I rejoice in his memory, and will not be so disloyal to it as to snivel over his valiant death. So tear up your mourning and hang up your brightest colours in his honour, and let us all praise God that he did not die in a snuffy bed of a trumpery cough, weakened by age and saddened by the disappointments that would have attended his work had he lived.

Eamon de Valera

The dominant political figure in twentieth-century Ireland, de Valera was born in New York in 1882 to a Spanish father and Irish mother. He was reared by his maternal grandmother in rural Co. Limerick, studied mathematics at the Royal University and worked as a teacher. In 1908, he joined the Gaelic League, beginning a lifelong devotion to the Irish language. He joined the Irish Volunteers on their formation in 1913 and was officer commanding one of the outlying garrisons during the 1916 Rising.

He was the only one of the garrison commanders not to be executed. The cause is disputed: there was heavy political pressure on the British authorities to stop the executions; de Valera's American citizenship may have saved him; it may even be that he was regarded as a marginal, unimportant figure. If the last was the case, it was one of the misjudgements of the century.

As the senior surviving commander, he now had matchless prestige. He assumed the leadership of Sinn Féin in 1917, was elected to the Dáil for East Clare and was arrested and jailed by the British for a trumped-up 'German Plot'. He escaped – Michael Collins organized this – and went to America to raise funds and to spread the gospel of Irish nationalism.

As the leader of the anti-treaty side which rejected the settlement with the British, he spent some time in jail, and emerged to find the new state established and himself in the political wilderness. By the mid-1920s, Sinn Féin had become the party of no-compromise republicanism. Despairing of its intransigence, de Valera founded his own less doctrinaire republican party, Fianna Fáil, in 1927. In 1932, the party was in government.

He proceeded to unpick what he regarded as the most objectionable provisions of the Anglo-Irish Treaty, introduced a new quasi-republican constitution in 1937 and maintained Irish neutrality during World War II. For this, he drew the hostility of Winston Churchill. Neutrality had overwhelming public support – the memory of Irish losses in World War I were still fresh – and it was a policy adopted by any European country that could get away with it. Dev did not help matters, however, by excessive punctilio, even going so far as to offer his condolences to the German ambassador on the death of Hitler.

Churchill attacked de Valera in an ungracious victory speech at the end of the war. Dev's reply was a masterpiece of restrained and dignified rhetoric. In fact, Irish wartime neutrality consistently showed 'a certain consideration for Britain'. For instance, British airmen who crash-landed in Ireland were spirited across the border to Northern Ireland; German pilots were interned. De Valera did nothing to prevent volunteers joining the British war effort, leading to the celebrated cartoon showing an all-Irish bomber crew avoiding anti-aircraft fire over Germany, with the pilot saying to the co-pilot 'Thank God Dev kept us out of all this.'

Fianna Fáil was in office from 1932 to 1948, from 1951 to 1954 and then from 1957 to 1973, utterly dominating the Irish political landscape. Its economic policy of protection behind tariff walls proved a failure in an era where the international drift was towards free trade, especially after 1945. De Valera's Ireland was conservative, with excessive deference shown to the Catholic Church and a social emphasis on rural rather than urban development. Divorce and contraception were banned, the literary censorship was ferocious to the point of stupidity, while frightening levels of emigration – especially in the 1950s – threatened the viability of the state.

De Valera retired from active politics in 1959 but immediately took up the ceremonial role of the presidency, which he held until 1973. He died two years later at the age of 93. His consuming ambitions – revival of the Irish language and the ending of partition – remained unfulfilled and seem as far away as ever today.

Ten Most Common Irish Surnames

Murphy	O'Brien
Kelly	Byrne
O'Sullivan	Ryan
Walsh	O'Connor
Smith	O'Neill

5

NATION, STATE AND PARISH PUMP

The Four Provinces

The four Irish provinces correspond roughly to the four cardinal points of the compass. According to legend, there was a fifth province in ancient Gaelic Ireland. The kingdom of Meath, comprising the modern county of that name plus a number of adjacent counties or parts of counties, was sometimes referred to as a fifth province. The name comes from the Old Irish *mide* meaning middle and the kingdom/province of Meath ran inland, north of the Dublin–Galway line and south of Ulster, as far as the River Shannon. However, whether kingdom or province, it need not concern us. We are dealing only with the four modern provinces.

LEINSTER

This is the eastern province, dominated by Dublin. The Irish capital is situated on the most accessible haven for shipping on the east coast, nearest to Britain. A mere glance at a map will demonstrate the truth of this. Even though the Boyne Valley to the immediate north was a centre of settled and sophisticated life from Neolithic times – Newgrange alone is evidence of that – the river itself creates no major harbour. In fact, it joins the sea in a rather modest confluence just east of the town of Drogheda.

Dublin Bay is another matter entirely. A grand C-shaped sweep, it offers an enticing invitation. It has its drawbacks: the bay is shallow, very tidal and prone to silting. But despite these vexations, it offered the quickest cross-channel passage to Britain, and thus Dublin, a Viking foundation, grew up around it.

The province of Leinster comprises the centre and south-east of the island east of the Shannon. Its northern boundary is set by the mountains, low hills and lakes that girdle the southern reaches of Ulster; to the east, there is the Irish Sea and to the west the Shannon, from which the inland boundary, separating it from Munster, runs in a roughly 45-degree angle to the south-east. This inland boundary marks two overlapping features of medieval Ireland: the greatest extent of English royal power (the so-called Pale) and the borderlands separating the great Norman lordships of the Butlers and the Fitzgeralds of Desmond (or Munster).

The Hiberno-Normans are important here. They first landed in what is now south Leinster, in Co. Wexford, and they settled the rich limestone land in which the province abounds. The prosperous river valleys of the south-east saw the densest Norman settlement; likewise the flat plains of what are now the counties of Meath, Westmeath and Kildare.

If you travel by train from Galway and nod off west of the Shannon only to wake up in Co. Kildare an hour or so later, you might be forgiven for thinking that you were in a different country.

More than two-thirds of the population of the Republic live in Leinster and nearly half in the Greater Dublin area. The statistics are telling:

Population of all Ireland (ROI & NI)	6,568,839
Population of ROI	4,756,972
Population of Leinster	3,422,957
Population of Greater Dublin area	2,137,639

The huge gravitational pull of Dublin is clear from another key statistic, available from the Irish Central Statistics Office. If we take a base figure of 100 to represent disposable income per person (excluding rent; figures for 2014), we see the following numbers just for Leinster alone, without ever venturing across provincial boundaries, where the results are even starker:

ROI	100
Dublin	110.1
Meath	96.7
South-East	94.5
Kilkenny	93.3
Offaly	89.2

In short, the further you move away from Dublin, the more the numbers weaken. Even prosperous areas like Meath, Kilkenny and the south-east show a marked gap relative to the capital. The small inland county of Offaly, bordering the Shannon, gives a hint of how that gap widens as one increases the distance from the capital.

Although Leinster, along with the other three provinces, has no administrative function (always allowing for the peculiar case of Northern Ireland), provincial loyalties are keenly felt. Until recent times, there was a belief that this provincial loyalty was weakest in the eastern province, and there may have been some merit to that speculation. What has put paid to it is the ferocious rivalry that has developed between the Leinster and Munster rugby teams.

Between them, they have won the premier European championship (formerly the Heineken Cup) five times in the twenty-first century, with Leinster holding the bragging rights, having three trophies to Munster's two. But Munster got there first, winning in 2006 and repeating the achievement in 2008, having lost two previous finals. The traditional contrast between the two provinces was that Munster played a tight, forward-dominated game whereas Leinster had a more expansive, running tradition. This led to a degree of Munster triumphalism, as their consistent superiority over Leinster led them to dub their neighbours 'the lady boys'. It rankled, so that when Leinster then displaced them as the leading Irish province and actually exceeded Munster's haul of trophies, they took considerable pleasure in it. The rivalry continues.

So, in an Irish context, province does count for something. It probably is more weakly expressed in Leinster than in the other three but there is a further reason for that: the rest of the country against Dublin. People don't need statistics, as above, to feel this ancient antagonism. For non-Dubliners, the city's population are 'jackeens', that is little John (Bull) or quasi-English in short. This name-calling is generally a bad idea where sharp-tongued city folk are concerned. For the Dubs, their country cousins are boggers and culchies. The latter term is variously glossed as deriving from the word 'agricultural' or possibly as a reference to the town of Kiltimagh, Co. Mayo (pron. Cul-cha mock), regarded by all true Dubs as the Back of God Speed.

The dominance of a capital city, relative to the rest of the country, is hardly a phenomenon unique to Ireland. One need only look east to observe the overweening position of London or the traditional whip hand that Paris has held over the rest of France. Relative to the province of Leinster, however, the Dublin problem is even more acute as the surrounding counties effectively become part of the Greater Dublin commuter belt. House prices in the capital have driven young couples, in particular, out to provincial towns and villages which now act in large part as exurbs that empty their working population into the capital each weekday morning.

So if Dublin holds all the best cards in Leinster, Leinster holds the strongest hand in Ireland. It has more good land than any other province, it is orientated to the east with one eye on the larger island adjacent, and while it is only the third-largest province by area – Munster and Ulster are bigger – it is by far the richest and most populous.

The twelve counties of Leinster, with their county towns:

Dublin	Dublin
Kildare	Naas
Wicklow	Wicklow
Wexford	Wexford
Kilkenny	Kilkenny
Carlow	Carlow
Laois	Portlaoise
Offaly	Tullamore
Westmeath	Mullingar
Longford	Longford
Meath	Navan
Louth	Drogheda

MUNSTER

The southern province, bounded on three sides by the sea and on the fourth by that diagonal separating it from Leinster that we noted earlier. There is one odd aspect of the province, however, and that is the presence of Co. Clare in it. A glance at a map would suggest that Clare belongs in Connacht, separated as it is from the rest of the province by the natural barrier of the Shannon estuary.

Indeed, I have a seventeenth-century map made by the cartographer Hommano of Nuremberg with the provinces colour-coded. Clare is very sensibly in with the rest of Connacht, where you feel it naturally belongs.

Despite shifting boundaries over the centuries – the present stable boundaries of the provinces only date from the seventeenth century – there was historically a sense of regional difference in what we now call Munster. In Gaelic Ireland, there was a rough division of the area between Thomond, the northern half, and Desmond, the southern. (That division has maintained a faint echo in modern times in the rivalry between the two principal cities in the province, Cork and Limerick.) At different times, various dynasties secured provincial overlordship from the great natural redoubt at the Rock of Cashel in Co. Tipperary. Eventually it was a Munster king, Brian Ború, who made the most plausible claim to the high kingship of Ireland in the early eleventh century.

As in Leinster, the rich agricultural land of central and southern Munster attracted the Normans. While parts of the province came under the sway of the Butlers, the earls of Ormond based in Kilkenny, the dominant family was the Fitzgeralds, known commonly as the Desmond Fitzgeralds because of their heartland in the south of the province. Their brittle relationship with the neighbouring Butlers was a running theme but the family destroyed itself and lost everything in the Reformation wars of the late sixteenth century. Disastrously, they appealed to the Pope against the crown of England. It proved a fatal mistake.

That opened up large parts of the province to adventurers from England who were planted on Fitzgerald lands forfeit to the crown. Of these, Richard Boyle, 1st Earl of Cork, was one of the best known. He was responsible for establishing or greatly improving many towns in Co. Cork and was a promoter of early industry. Among his enterprises were ironworks. These required charcoal, which Boyle produced by the simple expedient of cutting down much of the extensive woodland that still dominated the province.

It was this process at the hands of Boyle and others that prompted one of the most celebrated lines in Irish ballad poetry:

> *Cad a dhéanfaimid feasta gan adhmad*
> *Tá deireadh na gcoillte ar lár*

Or, in Frank O'Connor's translation, with Yeats' hand very visible:

> What shall we do for timber?
> The last of the woods is down.

The anonymous poet who composed those lines was not the last of his tribe and kind to show resentment of the newcomers. Munster had been a great centre for Gaelic schools of poetry, in which the poets depended on lordly patrons, Gaelic and Hiberno-Norman alike. Indeed, among the most famous Irish-language poets of the medieval era was one Gerald FitzMaurice FitzGerald (1335–98) known as *Gearóid Iarla*, or Gerald the Earl. And earl he was indeed, the 3rd Earl of Desmond, no less, head of one of the greatest Hiberno-Norman magnate families. Of all the great families, the Desmond Fitzgeralds adopted Gaelic language and customs more thoroughly than any other.

But by the early eighteenth century, the New English interest was dominant in Munster. To be fair, the modern appearance of the province owes much to their enterprise but that was cold comfort for the poets, who regarded the new men as parvenus, which they were, and boors. Abandoned by the destruction of the old order upon which they had relied, they had nothing left but rhetoric. It was, however, some rhetoric. No poet was more fluent or more bitter than Egan O'Rahilly (1670–1726) from Co. Kerry in the west of the province.

In 'A Grey Eye Weeping', he wrote:

> That my old bitter heart was pierced in this black doom,
> That foreign devils have made our land a tomb
> That the sun that was Munster's glory has gone down
> Has made me a beggar before you, Valentine Brown.

O'Rahilly would have regarded Valentine Brown, the new man on the make, as possessing a barbarous name. To the very end, O'Rahilly hurled defiance at the hated new order. These are the first and last stanzas of his magnificent 'Last Lines', old money talking to new:

> I shall not call for help until they coffin me –
> What good for me to call when hope of help is gone?
> Princes of Munster who would have heard my cry
> Will not rise from the dead because I am alone.
>
> ...
>
> Now I shall cease, death comes, and I must not delay
> By Laune and Laine and Lee, diminished of their pride,
> I shall go after the heroes, ay, into the clay –
> My fathers followed theirs before Christ was crucified.

(Translations by Frank O'Connor)

Despite the disappointments of the poets, the province prospered. The port of Youghal controlled most of the trade to the west of England. Kinsale was a major importer of tobacco, the Irish market for which seemed insatiable, and Cork itself had a vigorous trade with the continent. Over time, Cork took advantage of its central location and magnificent natural harbour to eclipse the smaller ports on either side of it and establish itself as the dominant regional entrepôt. The greater geographical range of Cork's maritime trade was very marked: in the 1680s, only a quarter of its trade was with England, almost as much as it was doing with the Caribbean islands, whereas the greatest proportion was with France, the Low Countries and the Iberian Peninsula.

It was the provision trade that came to dominate the commerce of the southern capital. Until about 1750, the principal commodities in the city's trade were beef, butter and woollens, in that order. The second half of the eighteenth century saw a dramatic expansion. The beef trade, in particular, flourished. As with beef, so went the butter trade, although not to the same volume or degree. From the 1760s onwards, this commercial expansion was driven by war.

It is an ill wind that blows no good. While war is generally bad for commerce, it is not always so. Britain was almost continually at war with France – and for a time with its own American colonies, which had French assistance – from the start of the Seven Years War in 1756 until the Battle of Waterloo in 1815. Intervals of peace were blessed remissions, but the whole period – the span of two adult lifetimes – was one of international conflict.

The long series of wars brought high prices for the staples that sustained Munster's prosperity, and Cork's in particular: beef and butter, as we have seen, and in time pork and bacon. Armies, as Napoleon knew, march on their stomachs, so they need to be fed. The rise in the production of Munster pork came from military demand. The relative ease with which pork can be salted and preserved made it ideal for the army.

Munster became one of the biggest centres of the provision trade in Europe, located as it was on the western margins of one of the principal military combatants. The province became the bread basket of the British Army, and Cork the port with the most developed supply infrastructure.

The Great Famine of the mid nineteenth century had as devastating an effect on Munster as on everywhere else outside east Ulster, which was saved by the industrial revolution. The greatest suffering occurred along the Atlantic seaboard, especially either side of the Shannon estuary and in the four south-western peninsulas that jut out like fingers into the ocean. Reports and images in the *Illustrated London News* from the West Cork town of Skibbereen and other western locales horrified contemporary opinion. While not as severe as in Connacht, population loss in Munster was high. Every county in the province suffered a population decline in the intercensal period 1841–51.

Munster recovered in time, sustained by the excellent agricultural land in its central counties. Cork and Limerick developed a modest industrial and commercial life. The gradual growth of tourism was centred on Killarney in Co. Kerry – heaven's reflex, according to a moniker that it never tires of. It is also the heartland of hurling, Ireland's national sport, which we noted earlier and of which more anon. However, the modern game has been dominated by Kilkenny, across the provincial border in Leinster.

Top Tourist Sites in Munster

Killarney
The West Cork peninsulas
The Ring of Kerry (Iveragh Peninsula)
Dingle and Slea Head (Dingle Peninsula, Co. Kerry)
The Cliffs of Moher, Co. Clare
The Burren, Co. Clare
The Rock of Cashel, Co. Tipperary

The Six Munster Counties with Their County Towns

Cork	Cork
Kerry	Tralee
Limerick	Limerick
Clare	Ennis
Tipperary	Nenagh
Waterford	Waterford

Connacht

The western province, Connacht, is basically surrounded by the Atlantic on three sides and bordered by the River Shannon to the east. There is a little bit of the province to the east of the river, in Co. Leitrim, a reminder that in medieval times Connacht was more extensive, reaching into what is today a part of south-west Ulster and also into Co. Longford, now in Leinster. This was known as the rough third of Connacht.

The province has had a good and a bad press; ironically, two sides of the same coin. Cromwell famously offered dispossessed Catholic landowners in Munster and Leinster the chance to go 'to Hell or to Connacht', seeing it as a sort of remote and impoverished wilderness. It was anything but, having a developed commercial life by the standards of the time. For centuries, Galway was the second most important port in Ireland. But, that said, Connacht has less good agricultural land than the other three provinces.

It is common simply to refer to it as the West of Ireland, as if Clare, Kerry and Cork did not exist. But this too reflects a mindset. If Dublin is psychologically orientated to the east – gazing towards England – then mentally this place away to the west is at the back door, something of a place apart. It can seem either a conservative and backward fastness or the most authentic part of Ireland, a place that gives the truest expression to the national character. Take your pick, according to inclination.

Connacht is the least urbanized of the Irish provinces. While Galway is the fourth-largest city in the Republic of Ireland, the next-largest town, Sligo, is ranked 24th. There are many small towns and villages but there is less urban development here than elsewhere.

Although it has the poorest land, it still attracted the Normans. The de Burgo family, ancestors of the modern Burkes, established themselves in the province in the thirteenth century, displacing the Gaelic O'Connors – who at one stage had aspired to the high kingship – from many of their strongholds. The family divided the province between two branches based in Co. Mayo, where the anglicized spelling was usually Bourke, and the Co. Galway branch, where the spelling was the simpler Burke, although – just to complicate the thing – they also answered to the name of Clanrickarde.

The de Burgos established a leading position in medieval Connacht, but they had to coexist with the Gaelic lordships. In the late sixteenth century, one of the family became the second husband of the remarkable Grace O'Malley, famed for her adventures as a dashing sea captain. Her family was based on the coast of Mayo and its adjacent islands and she was recognized by the English administration as a formidable and able power in the region. She commanded the loyalty of hundreds of men and had at her disposal a fleet of ships. In 1593, she sailed from Mayo to London to meet Queen Elizabeth and had her petition to the queen granted. She was one of the most remarkable women in Irish history.

Galway city owes its existence to the southern branch of the Burkes, who founded a castle there in the thirteenth century. It developed into an important port, trading in particular with Spain. This is commemorated in the so-called Spanish Arch, actually part of the old city wall dating from the 1580s. The wall was destroyed in the most improbable circumstances in 1755: a tsunami that followed the great Lisbon earthquake of that year made it all the way to Galway, a distance of over 1,600 km, and swept away most of the wall.

The modern city is a vibrant place, a university city with a number of other institutes of higher education, a major regional hospital and an expanded industrial and commercial base. It is also the gateway to the beautiful wilderness of Connemara, one of Ireland's leading tourist areas.

In Co. Mayo, to the north of Galway, there are a number of pleasant towns of which the finest is Westport, an estate town laid out in the eighteenth century. Offshore is Clew Bay, said to contain an island for every day of the year and just to the west of the town is Croagh Patrick, where according to legend St Patrick fasted for forty days and forty nights. It is the site of a long-established pilgrimage, for on the last Sunday of every July pilgrims climb the mountain – or the Reek, as it is commonly styled – some of them barefoot. There is a church at the summit.

On the northern coast of Co. Mayo lies one of the most remarkable archaeological sites in Ireland, the Céide Fields. A brilliant example of painstaking fieldwork has exposed a tract of Neolithic farms, complete with boundary walls and markers. The site is dated to about 3000 BC and its recovery was made possible by the preservative properties of the blanket bog that subsequently covered it. The whole area exposed covers more than 10 sq km.

Further north again, the county of Sligo is indelibly associated with W.B. Yeats and contains many sites made memorable by his poetry: the mountains of Ben Bulben and Knocknarea; the lake isle of Innisfree; Rosses Point and Lissadell House. The poet is buried in the churchyard at Drumcliff, just north of Sligo town on the main road north to Co. Donegal, 'under bare Ben Bulben's head'.

To the east of Co. Sligo lies Co. Leitrim, one of the poorest counties in Ireland. It is the only part of Connacht with land lying east of the Shannon and in reality the county is dominated by the river and its associated lakes. The Shannon is the longest river in the British Isles. It rises in the neighbouring Co. Cavan and is already an impressive waterway by the time it has reached Carrick-on-Shannon, the county town. This is a popular starting point for those who take leisure cruisers on the big river.

South of Co. Leitrim, the river girdles the eastern boundary of Roscommon, the fifth county of Connacht, and also forms the provincial boundary with Leinster. For Irish people, the idea of crossing the Shannon – especially when going west into Connacht – provides a mild frisson, as though one is moving from one world to another. As per the myths associated with the province, some regard this as a regressive step. But such persons are well outnumbered by those who love the western province, with its mixture of wildness and intimacy, its historical associations and its sense of distance from the bustling world.

Top Tourist Sites in Connacht

Galway City
Connemara, Co. Galway
Westport and Clew Bay, Co. Mayo
Achill Island, Co. Mayo
Céide Fields, Downpatrick Head, Co. Mayo
Sligo town and environs

The Five Counties of Connacht with Their County Towns

Galway	Galway
Mayo	Castlebar
Sligo	Sligo
Leitrim	Carrick-on-Shannon
Roscommon	Roscommon

Ulster

The northern province. In modern times, its name is known worldwide for all the wrong reasons. But while it has a long history, it is best understood through geography. The twin keys to Ulster are its proximity to Scotland and the series of low hills – called drumlins – and lakes that protect its southern boundary and make access from the south difficult.

Because of this latter fact, Ulster was for many centuries the most remote and self-contained of the Irish provinces. Even today, there is a limited number of access points from the south. The best-known of these, the Moyry Pass between Dundalk, Co. Louth and Newry, Co. Down, carries both the Dublin–Belfast motorway and the railway line. It also makes southern Ulster classic ambush territory, a tradition that stretches from Hugh O'Neill in the 1590s to the IRA during the recent troubles.

This inaccessibility meant that Ulster saw less of the Normans than the other provinces, although one John de Courcy did push through the Moyry Pass in 1177 and built the immense castle of Carrickfergus, just north of present-day Belfast. This Norman colony never established itself as securely as lordships elsewhere and was subject to harassment by Gaelic families. It never completely disappeared, however, if only because Carrickfergus was invulnerable to Gaelic arms. Moreover, the Normans retained a toehold on the southern shore of Belfast Lough.

But overall, Ulster remained the most Gaelic part of Ireland until the final defeat of its Gaelic lords in 1603.

The second salient geographical fact is the province's proximity to Britain, specifically to Scotland. At the narrowest point, it is barely 20 km from the north-east coast to the Mull of Kintyre. Indeed, for centuries there existed a seaborne kingdom called Dal Riada on either side of the water, in what is now north Co. Antrim and in Argyll on the Scottish shore. The historic links between east Ulster and Scotland did not have to await the seventeenth-century plantations; they had been there since antiquity. The most obvious example is on the island of Iona, the monastic site on which was founded by the Irishman St Columba, who introduced Christianity to Scotland in the sixth century.

Of course, the plantations gave a radical new twist to this old theme and transformed the province, with consequences that persist to the present day. But the long-established commerce between Ulster and Scotland inclined the province's gaze away from the rest of Ireland and outward to the larger island. This was compounded by the difficulty of overland travel – not just all those hills and lakes to the south but also the problems of overland travel everywhere before the age of modern road engineering.

If the land was a barrier, the sea was a highway. In modern times, we think of it the other way round. But historically, that was the reality. People in Ulster were far better acquainted with western Scotland and its islands than they were with Munster. That situation too was compounded by the plantations.

There is one particularly pleasing exception to this rule. Not only has modern road-building come to Ulster as to everywhere else in the developed world; it has also provided the province with the only true corniche in Ireland. The Antrim Coast Road runs between the towns of Larne and Ballycastle and is a thing of true beauty. It was built in the nineteenth century to open up the hitherto inaccessible Glens of Antrim.

Not far from Portrush to the west along the North Antrim Coast lies the Giant's Causeway, Ulster's only World Heritage Site.

Internally, the province falls naturally into four sub-regions. East and west of the River Bann, which flows from south to north, lie the most populated areas. To the east, the counties of Antrim and Down are dominated by the city of Belfast. To the west as far as the estuary of the River Foyle, the central part of the province was the historic heartland of O'Neill power. The principal city is Derry. Beyond the Foyle lies the rugged mountain terrain of Co. Donegal, and we have already noted the fourth sub-region, the southern borderlands.

Ulster east of the Bann was the only part of Ireland to experience the industrial revolution. In the nineteenth century, the population of Belfast grew from fewer than 30,000 in 1800 to more than 300,000 in 1900. Shipbuilding, textiles, tobacco and engineering were the powerhouses of Ulster's industrial economy. Of all the enterprises, none was more famous than the shipyard of Harland & Wolff, which built the most famous ship ever to sail and sink, the *Titanic*.

The huge and sudden growth in Belfast's population meant an influx of new workers from the countryside to the city. Sadly, they brought with them some of the sectarian animosities that had been a feature of rural Ulster since plantation days. Mutual suspicion and distrust, sometimes breaking out in open hatred and murder, between Catholic and Protestant became firmly embedded in the life of the province. Even among Protestants, there was little affection between Anglican and Presbyterian.

The sad story of the Northern Ireland troubles has been told a thousand times and it seems pointless to rehearse it here. As I write, the relative stability that has been achieved by the peace process is threatened by Brexit, the decision taken by plebiscite in the UK to leave the European Union. It threatens the reintroduction of a hard border, complete with border checkpoints, between the Republic and Northern Ireland, an echo of the bad old days. Since the peace agreements were signed, you only notice that you have moved from one jurisdiction to the other when the distance signs change from metric to imperial or vice versa.

There are nine counties in Ulster, more than any other province except Leinster. Of these, six comprise Northern Ireland while three are in the Republic. The line of partition was drawn on crude sectarian grounds, securing the largest geographical area that could command a Protestant and Unionist majority. Even at that, the area west of the Bann has a Catholic/nationalist majority, so that Northern Ireland is a house divided.

One of the ironies of partition is that Co. Donegal, which is the most northerly county on the island, is in the South. Its beautiful mountain and coastal scenery and its stunning beaches make it a playground for every sort of person from across the border. And although it may be in the Republic, it is beyond question an Ulster county. Accent, dialect and disposition all attest to that.

Top Tourist Attractions in Ulster

The Giant's Causeway, Co. Antrim
The Titanic Museum, Belfast
Carrick-a-Rede Rope Bridge, Co. Antrim
Dunluce Castle, Co. Antrim
Mount Stewart, Co. Down
Castle Coole, Co. Fermanagh
Armagh city
Upper & Lower Lough Erne, Co. Fermanagh
Carrickfergus Castle, Co. Antrim
Antrim Coast Road, from Larne to Ballycastle
The Glens of Antrim
The Walls of Derry
The Grianan of Aileach, Co. Donegal
The Inishowen Peninsula, Co. Donegal

The Nine Counties of Ulster with Their County Towns

Antrim	Belfast
Down	Downpatrick
Donegal	Lifford
Tyrone	Omagh
Armagh	Armagh
Fermanagh	Enniskillen
Monaghan	Clones
Cavan	Cavan
Derry	Derry

Northern Ireland

Let's keep this short. There have been whole libraries of books published about NI. There is little to add and almost nothing new to say.

Until the 1600s, nearly all of Ulster was solidly Gaelic. The exception was a small private plantation scheme in the two eastern counties of Antrim and Down, parts of which were settled by British Protestants. This was hugely compounded by the official Plantation of Ulster that followed the military crushing of the Gaelic lords. It continued through the entire seventeenth century, involving one of the largest population transfers in contemporary Europe.

The effect was to turn central and eastern Ulster into Protestant strongholds. Although some Protestants – mainly Presbyterians – flirted briefly with the principles of the French Revolution, the failed rising of 1798 ended that rather abruptly. In the nineteenth century, the advance of Catholic nationalism in the other three provinces and the success of the industrial revolution in Protestant Ulster opened a division that has never been healed.

Ulster Protestants feared Catholic dominance – 'home rule is Rome rule' – and mobilized against successive home rule bills.

When the third such bill became law in 1914, Ireland was on the brink of civil war. Then the act was suspended for the duration of World War I. In 1916, the Easter Rising and the Battle of the Somme occurred within weeks of each other. Ulster troops died in huge numbers on the Somme: their sacrifice was contrasted with what was regarded as an act of gross treachery in time of war.

When the war ended, the southern nationalist demand hardened, as did unionist resistance. Irresistible force met immovable object. The result was partition, with the new state of Northern Ireland still part of the UK. NI was carved out of the largest slice of Ulster that guaranteed a Protestant and unionist majority. The settlement has never been accepted by the large nationalist minority. Sporadic attacks on the institutions of the new state culminated in the outbreak of the 'troubles' in 1968. It took until 2006 to get a kind of permanent ceasefire. Despite all the mayhem, the basic constitutional position remains unchanged.

Political and Electoral Systems

In ROI, the three branches of government are the President, the Dáil (lower house of parliament) and the Seanad or Senate (upper house).

The President is elected by universal suffrage, with the vote available to all over the age of 18. The Dáil, comprising 158 deputies, is elected by proportional representation using the single transferrable vote (PR-STV), which is the system that produces results proportionate to the wishes of the electorate, as measured by their first preferences. There are 40 multi-seat constituencies, with either three, four or five seats in each. Voters rank the candidates in order of preference, number 1 being the first choice, and so on down. They can therefore give a numbered preference to every candidate in the constituency if they choose; otherwise, they can stop after their first preference or at any point. A recent proposal, if acted upon, will increase the number of TDs to 160, elected from 39 constituencies.

In each constituency, the returning officer determines the quota of votes that successful candidates must reach, using an established formula. Candidates who are elected then have their surplus – the difference between their final figure and the quota – distributed by allocating their lower preferences. Likewise, no-hope candidates at the bottom of the poll are eliminated and their lower preferences distributed.

This entails many counts – it is common, for instance, for nobody to be elected on the first count – and can drag on for days in the five-seaters. It sounds complicated, especially if you are accustomed to the brutal clarity of the first-past-the-post system. In fact, it is generally easy to understand – a few technical details notwithstanding – and it has widespread public support. The slow business of counting paper votes makes for riveting television – a kind of electoral Grand National.

If the upside of PR is fairness, the downside is the potential for instability. The 2016 general election was a particular case in point, with a large number of independents and localists returned, which made government formation difficult. Historically, however, this has been less of a problem.

The Seanad is elected by a number of vocational panels, whose electorates comprise members of local authorities. In addition, the graduates of the two leading universities elect three senators each. The Taoiseach (Prime Minister) has the right of personal nomination of eleven, bringing the full senatorial complement to sixty.

The Taoiseach is elected by the Dáil and is generally the leader of the largest party. He appoints the cabinet, each of whom receives his or her seal of office from the President. The President's functions are largely symbolic and ceremonial but he or she can refer proposed legislation to the higher courts to test its constitutionality.

The constitution dates from 1937 with subsequent amendments made by referendum (see p. 201).

In NI, the first-past-the-post system copper-fastened Unionist hegemony for many years. Under the pressure of the early troubles, PR-STV was introduced in 1973. For many years, the Ulster Unionist

Party was the principal Protestant voice and the Social Democratic and Labour Party (SDLP) the majority nationalist group. The respective minority groups were the Democratic Unionist Party (DUP), the vehicle of the demagogue Ian Paisley, and Sinn Féin, the mouthpiece of the IRA.

With the signing of the Belfast Agreement of 1998, which ended the worst of the troubles, the party positions inverted. Not only did the DUP and Sinn Féin come to dominate their respective electorates, these bitter opposites actually entered into a power-sharing executive. It is a rickety structure, hardly sustained by mutual esteem, but it is better than what had gone before.

Political Parties Explained

In ROI until recent times, there was what was commonly called the two-and-a-half party system. The 'two and a half parties' were Fianna Fáil, Fine Gael and Labour. Let's look at them in turn.

FIANNA FÁIL (pron. Fee-anna Fall, generally translated as the Soldiers of Destiny) was de Valera's party and it dominated the Irish political landscape from 1932 until 2011. It governed alone from 1932 until 1989 – with a few interruptions – and subsequently as the dominant party in coalitions.

FF is a constitutional republican party. It emerged out of the losing side in the civil war of 1922–23. It regards itself as a national movement not merely a party; it has always seen itself as the nation in embryo. It is populist and although generally orthodox on economic matters, it makes the occasional gesture to the left. It was traditionally a supporter of semi-state (nationalized) enterprises and public housing schemes. Its self-image is that it is the party of the people. Until it fell apart in the 2011 election following the financial crash, traditionally it was one of the most formidable party machines anywhere.

FINE GAEL (pron. Fin-eh Gale, generally translated as the Family of the Irish) emerged from the winning side in the civil war. If FF is a party of the people, FG is more the party of the state. After all, its predecessors established the state. It is less populist than FF, more orthodox in economics, with fewer flirtations with populist bromides, and more rooted in the urban middle class and the larger farmers.

So the two main parties are basically conservative, reflecting their electorates. However, the social changes of the last twenty or so years have shaken the stability of the traditional structures, especially with the emergence of a populist working-class movement and the arrival of Sinn Féin as a serious political force in ROI, these being in many respects two sides of the same coin. It has meant an unhappy time for the 'half party' in the two-and-a-half-party system, Labour.

THE LABOUR PARTY is older than the state. It was formed in 1912 and its periods in office have usually been as a junior coalition partner of FG on the few occasions when FF were voted out. For most of its life it has, basically, been the political extension of the trade union movement, depending on urban working-class votes (although FF usually did better among this social group) and rural labourers, the sort that might be employed by the big farmers in FG.

From the 1960s on, Labour attracted some urban intellectuals and ran in the 1969 general election on what was by Irish standards a startlingly left-wing programme under the slogan 'The 70s will be socialist'. To this, FF replied that the socialists will be 70 – and they proved to be nearer the mark. Labour, even in its better years, has never won 40 seats in the Dáil. Its best years were 1992 (33 seats) and 2011 (37 seats in the year of the FF meltdown). However, they suffered badly for their participation in the government formed in 2011 – again in junior partnership with FG – being blamed for austerity policies that fell heaviest on their natural constituency. In 2016, they were reduced to a mere seven seats.

The space vacated by FF, still recovering slowly from the 2011 debacle but nowhere near their old selves, and by Labour has been filled by Sinn Féin and various populists and independents. Between them, they ensured that government formation after the 2016 election was the most difficult in the history of the state.

Localism

No discussion of Irish public life can ignore this phenomenon. It's hardly an accident that it was an Irish-American politician, Tip O'Neill, who coined the phrase that 'all politics is local'. The PR-STV system facilitates localism, although it hardly invented it. It goes back to British days. But it means that a candidate can be returned to the Dáil on purely parish-pump issues. The threatened closure of a local hospital in favour of a bigger regional one is such a pressure point. There are many others.

PR-STV accentuates localism in this manner. A party has a reasonably predictable slate of votes in a given constituency. But in a desire to win as many seats as possible, it will usually run more than one candidate. At worst, if one of them loses, his or her transfers will stay with the party to boost the remaining party candidates.

All this means that as a candidate your principal enemy is in your own party, vying for the biggest share of the party slate. It is common for candidates to be chosen for the local bailiwicks they can command, so that the party vote can be maximized in the constituency. It is considered bad form – although by no means unknown – for candidates who are feeling the heat or who are simply bloody-minded to 'invade' another's bailiwick to poach votes there.

The successful politician cultivates his local patch assiduously and woe betide him at the next election if he doesn't. Regular clinics, involvement in highly visible voluntary activity such as sports clubs, attending funerals and generally being at the beck and call of the electorate is hardly designed to raise your gaze towards the far horizons. Rather, it keeps you concentrated firmly on the parish pump, which is exactly where the electors want you to be. The net effect is a mixture of localism and populism in which the deputy's principal job is regarded as mediating between individual constituents and the apparatus of the state.

The potential for corruption in this process is considerable. In planning matters, where serious sums of money can be involved, it has been the cause of a number of scandals. The Irish electorate, like electorates everywhere, grumbles about its public representatives, but basically regards them as messenger boys and girls delivering for the down-home parish. If you make it to the cabinet the pressure increases, in the belief that now you can really deliver good stuff – transport links, rural broadband, what have you. Budding statesmen are hardly encouraged by this system.

Ten Irish Political Quotations

'For legal and professional reasons neither myself nor my advisors have been in a position to respond to any of the accuracy and completeness of the reports about those issues so it is not correct, if I said so I wasn't correct, so I, I can't recall if I did say, but I did not say, if I did say it I didn't mean to say it that these issues could not be dealt with until the end of the Mahon Tribunal, that is not what Revenue said.'
Bertie Ahern, Taoiseach 1997–2008, clarifying things in the Dáil concerning matters being examined by a tribunal of inquiry

'Among the best traitors Ireland has ever had, Mother Church ranks at the very top, a massive obstacle in the path to equality and freedom. She has been a force for conservatism ... to ward off threats to her own security and influence.'
Bernadette Devlin

'No man has the right to fix the boundary of the march of a nation. No man has the right to say to his country "thus far shalt thou go

and no further" and we have never attempted to fix the *ne plus ultra* to the progress of Ireland's nationhood and we never shall.'
Charles Stewart Parnell

'If the word "no" was removed from the English language, Ian Paisley would be speechless.'
John Hume

'Not for all the universe contains would I, in the struggle for what I conceive my country's cause, consent to the effusion of a single drop of human blood, except my own.'
Daniel O'Connell

'Think, what have I got for Ireland? Something which she has wanted these past seven hundred years. Will anyone be satisfied with the bargain? Will anyone? I tell you this – this morning I signed my death warrant. I thought at the time how odd, how ridiculous – a bullet may just as well have done the job five years ago.'
Michael Collins, on signing the Anglo-Irish Treaty 1921

'Mr Churchill is proud of Britain's stand alone after France had fallen and before America entered the war. Could he not find in his heart the generosity to acknowledge that there is a small nation that stood alone, not for one year or two, but for several hundred years against aggression; that endured spoliations, famines, massacres, in endless succession; that was clubbed many times into insensibility but each time on regaining consciousness, took up the fight anew; a small nation that could never be got to accept defeat and has never surrendered her soul?'
Éamon de Valera, in response to a broadcast by Churchill critical of Ireland's wartime neutrality, 1945

'Let no man write my epitaph; for as no man who knows my motives dare now vindicate them, let not prejudice or ignorance asperse them. Let them rest in obscurity and peace. Let my memory be left in oblivion, my tomb remain uninscribed, until other times and other men can do justice to my character. When

my country takes her place among the nations of the earth, then and not till then let my epitaph be written.'
Robert Emmet, under sentence of death for
his rebellion, 1803

'Let us hope and trust that there are sufficient proud and ignorant people left in this country to stand up to the intellectuals who are out to destroy faith and fatherland.'
Oliver J. Flanagan, populist backbench TD, 1971

'Life springs from death and from the graves of patriot men and women spring living nations. The defenders of this realm have worked well in secret and in the open. They think that they have pacified Ireland. They think that they have purchased half of us and intimidated the other half. They think that they have foreseen everything, think that they have provided against everything; but the fools, the fools, the fools, they have left us our Fenian dead and while Ireland holds these graves Ireland unfree shall never be at peace.'
Patrick Pearse, at the grave of the old Fenian
Jeremiah O'Donovan Rossa, 1915

6

IRISH ENGLISH / ENGLISH IRISH

The back-and-forth relationship between Ireland and Britain has been dictated by geography. In addition, the gravitational pull of the more powerful and richer large island has been a substantial factor. In this chapter, we look at some people, born in Ireland, who made a significant contribution to British life. We have already mentioned St Patrick, who made the traffic in the other direction, and we could add some later English names who left their mark on Ireland.

Richard Boyle, 1st Earl of Cork, was the most successful of the early Elizabethan adventurers, ending up as the richest man in Ireland and one who was able to lend the enormous sum of £15,000 to King Charles I in the 1620s. He was neither the first nor the last Englishman to make his mark in Ireland but as a general rule the traffic was in the other direction and that is where this chapter will concentrate its focus.

―――

Some Irish Who Made Their Mark Across the Water

―――

EDMUND BURKE

Burke was born in Dublin in 1729, the son of a lawyer. His family were Old English with roots in Co. Cork. It is supposed that his father's family had been Catholic but that Burke senior had conformed to the Established Church: he could not have practised law otherwise. After an education at Trinity College Dublin, Burke moved to London and enrolled in the Middle Temple. He became part of Dr Samuel Johnson's set; Johnson, not one to suffer fools, reputedly said of Burke that 'you could not stand five minutes with that man beneath a shed while it rained, but you had been convinced you were standing with the greatest man you had ever yet seen'.

However, it was as a writer and a politician that he distinguished himself rather than as a lawyer. In 1757 he published a well-received book on aesthetics entitled *A Philosophical Enquiry into the Origin of Our Ideas of the Sublime and Beautiful*. In 1765, he was elected to the House of Commons. He supported the rebellious American colonists as well as the loosening of restrictions on Catholics in Ireland. In the 1780s he was prominent in the unsuccessful attempt to impeach Warren Hastings, the former Governor General of Bengal, on charges of corruption.

In 1774, he wrote a famous letter to his constituents in Bristol, setting out in classic terms the need for an MP to retain his independence of thought and judgment: 'Your representative owes you, not his industry only, but his judgment; and he betrays, instead of serving you, if he sacrifices it to your opinion.' It cost him his seat in 1780, although he soon found another – or rather it was found for him, and he sat now for a pocket borough in Yorkshire in the gift of the Marquis of Rockingham.

Burke was therefore, by the standards of the day, a liberal and indeed his political allegiance lay with the faction known as the Rockingham Whigs, of whom the best known was Charles James Fox. It came as a considerable surprise when he broke with Fox over the events of the French Revolution. In general, Fox welcomed the early revolution but Burke was thoroughly alarmed by it. He wrote his most famous work, *Reflections on the Revolution in France* in 1790, prompting Tom Paine's celebrated response, *The Rights of Man*, the following year.

It was thus that Burke, who for most of his political career had been suspicious of royal authority, now produced the most famous defence of it. His work became an important intellectual source of Tory thought in the maelstrom of the Revolutionary and Napoleonic wars that lasted until 1815. By then, Burke was long gone: he died in 1797. His place as 'The father of Conservative (Tory) thinking' is too simple a summary for the career of a very remarkable man. But there is no doubt that the ideas and the values that he championed in *Reflections* had a lasting influence on the evolving philosophy of the Tory Party.

OLIVER GOLDSMITH

Two statues stand at the front gate of Trinity on College Green in Dublin. One is of Burke, the other of Goldsmith.

Oliver Goldsmith, poet, playwright, novelist and jobbing man of letters, was the son of a clergyman. As the statue suggests, he was a Trinity man and later studied medicine at Edinburgh and at Leyden in the Netherlands. He arrived in London a little later than Burke, in 1756, combining the practice of medicine with Grub Street scribbling. He too became part of the social and literary scene centred on Dr Johnson.

In 1766, he published the first of the works that made his name and reputation, the novel *The Vicar of Wakefield*. It mixes sentimental melodrama with acute social observation. But, as with all Goldsmith's best work, it was the easy charm of the writing that seduced the reader. In 1768, his first play, *The Good-Natur'd Man*, was produced at Covent Garden, having been declined by Garrick at Drury Lane.

In 1770, he published his most enduring work of verse, *The Deserted Village*, in which he recalls the innocent days of his childhood in Co. Longford while contrasting them with the cruelties caused in the contemporary English countryside by the growing practice of the enclosure of land. The lines 'Ill fares the land, to hastening ills a prey, / where wealth accumulates, and men decay' even possess an echo today among critics of globalization.

Goldsmith's supreme literary achievement was his second play, *She Stoops to Conquer*, one of the imperishable comedies in the English theatrical canon. Centring on a case of mischievous mistaken identity, which may be based on a trick played on young Goldsmith back in Ireland, it is both very funny and a mordant commentary on contemporary English manners and mores, not least to do with that perennial English social chestnut, class. As in all the best comedies, everything is resolved in the end, the confusions fall away and the appropriate marriages are arranged.

His recollections of Ireland were not central to his work, although they did inform *The Deserted Village* and he did write on a few other Irish themes, including an essay on the famous blind harper Turlough O'Carolan, a contemporary celebrity.

Goldsmith died in London in 1774, aged only 46. He was much loved. Even though he and Johnson had had a difference of opinion towards the end of his life, it was Johnson who composed the Latin epitaph for Goldsmith's memorial in Westminster Abbey. In English, it reads: 'There was almost no subject he did not write about, and he wrote about nothing without enhancing it.' Even better was his comment that 'no man was more foolish when he had not a pen in his hand, or more wise when he had'.

RICHARD BRINSLEY SHERIDAN

Was Sheridan Irish at all? It's a teasing question because the word 'Irish' did not carry the same weight of meaning in a pre-nationalist age as it does today. In the eighteenth century, this was especially true for Irish people born into the Anglican tradition, as Sheridan was. Ireland was a sister kingdom of Britain until the Act of Union (1801) but also part of a common culture, based on language, religious allegiance and a shared musical and literary environment. When nationalism developed later, the words 'Irish' and 'English' came to imply a greater degree of difference.

Richard Brinsley Sheridan was born in Ireland in 1751, to a well-known family. His father was a theatre manager and his mother a novelist and playwright. His paternal grandfather had been part of the circle centred on Jonathan Swift, just as the grandson would be a conspicuous member of the wits and intellects that orbited Dr Johnson in London. However, Sheridan left Ireland at the age of eight, never to return. He moved from a province to the metropole, rather as Johnson did when he came to London from Lichfield.

He was educated at Harrow, where he made no great impression. His public life began at Bath when he was in his early twenties. There he wooed and wed Elizabeth Linley, a famous beauty and singer known as The Maid of Bath. The courtship was a tangled business, eventually culminating in elopement; he based some of his later drama on its twists and turns.

In debt and generally stressed financially – he had already had to run off to France to avoid creditors – Sheridan's real passion was for politics. His playwriting and theatre management were primarily intended to help fund his political career. He was elected to parliament in 1780 for the constituency of Stafford, attaching himself to the Whig interest. This brought him into contact with Edmund Burke, with whom he later differed. Although his abilities were recognized, he gained little preferment from the Whig leadership.

Sheridan's enduring fame is as a playwright. Two of his plays, *The Rivals* and *The School for Scandal*, are among the greatest comedies in the English language. Like his father, he became a theatre manager and eventually bought Drury Lane Theatre from David Garrick in 1776. Over a number of years, he more than doubled its audience capacity but the costs involved were ruinous and his financial affairs were a permanent mess.

When Drury Lane burned down in 1809, his creditors – they were many – closed in. With typical wit, Sheridan sat in a nearby pub watching the theatre burn, saying 'a man can surely take a glass of wine by his own fireside'. He lost his seat in parliament and was finally arrested for debt. He died impoverished in 1816.

So, was Sheridan Irish other than in a nominal way? It is the old saw attributed to the Duke of Wellington that a cat born in a stable is not a horse. He wrote in an English comic idiom, with few references to Ireland. His best-known Irish character, Sir Lucius O'Trigger of Blunderbuss Hall in *The Rivals*, is not enough to claim him for Ireland. Were it so, we could claim Shakespeare on the basis of Macmorris in *Henry V*.

Still, Sheridan's comedies are in a recognizably outsider tradition that playwrights from Irish backgrounds excelled in, from Farquhar and Congreve in the late seventeenth century to Oscar Wilde and Shaw two centuries later. The outsider can mock the manners and mores of the metropole while still positioning himself, both by choice and ambition, as an insider. Do all comic dramatists do this to a greater or lesser extent? Perhaps, but it seems telling that this consistent insider–outsider tradition should be so well developed among playwrights of Irish background across such a long span of time.

Was it the greater distance of Ireland from London? Unlike any other recognizable nation or region within Great Britain – Scotland, Yorkshire, Wales – the degree of mental separation was greater in the Irish case: the Irish Sea reinforced it. In that sense, Richard

Brinsley Sheridan was more than just nominally Irish. His political and theatrical careers may have ended in failure and hopeless indebtedness but he has left us two plays of imperishable quality – and they are part of an explicitly Anglo-Irish dramatic continuity. That seems good enough.

JONATHAN SWIFT

Everyone mentioned in this chapter, with one exception, moved from Ireland to England to further his career. It was a one-way journey for all ambitious provincials, except for Swift. He certainly tried to make the conventional journey, and succeeded for a while, but when his ambition in London was frustrated he was obliged to return to Ireland, there to see out his career. For him, it was like an exile. He described it as 'a passage to the land I hate'.

Jonathan Swift was born in Dublin in 1667 and educated at Kilkenny College and Trinity. Like many Anglicans, he went to London at the time of the Jacobite revival in Ireland (1688–91) when it seemed that a Roman Catholic restoration was a real possibility. In 1691, he gained employment as secretary to Sir William Temple who lived at Moor Park near Farnham in Surrey. Temple was a retired Whig diplomat who had, among other manoeuvres, helped to arrange the marriage of William of Orange to Mary Stuart, the daughter of King James II. He was, therefore, one of the architects of the Glorious Revolution of 1688 that deposed James and put the staunchly Protestant William and Mary on the throne of England.

Temple was also a man of letters and Swift was set to work editing his essays. This immersion in the mind of a sophisticated man of the world who was perforce a flinty realist rubbed off on Swift and equipped him with mental qualities and attitudes – mixed with a misanthropy that came naturally to him – that turned him in time into the greatest satirist in the English language.

While at Moor Park, he met one of the two women whom he loved – albeit every possible ambiguity surrounds the manner in which Swift's loves found expression. Her name was Esther Johnson, although Swift has immortalized her as Stella. Although only a child when they first met – she had been born in 1681 – she grew into a beautiful young woman and remained close to Swift until her death in 1728. It has been speculated that they married in secret but this is disputed and the truth will never be known.

Swift returned briefly to Ireland in the late 1690s, having been ordained a priest in the Church of Ireland. He was awarded the parish of Kilroot, Co. Antrim, deep in Presbyterian territory. He developed a dislike of Presbyterians, and Calvinism generally, as great as that which he felt for Roman Catholicism. After a couple of years he was back in the more agreeable surrounds of Moor Park, where he remained until Sir William Temple's death in 1699.

The Kilroot years were, however, in no sense wasted. They inspired A Tale of a Tub, his first great satire, aimed principally at what he regarded as the vanity and conceit of Calvinism. Against the dogmatism of the Calvinists, he asserted the virtues of liberty and freedom of thought. He was, however, perfectly capable of his own evasions in these matters, for he was by conviction a Tory. That meant a commitment to legitimate regnal succession; in short, support for the Stuarts and suspicion of – if not outright opposition to – the Whig settlement in place since 1688. Dangerous ground. One man's liberty could be another's licence.

He gravitated to this position slowly, having previously had the instincts of a Whig for whom the Glorious Revolution had indeed been a deliverance. None the less, by 1710, he was firmly in the Tory camp and a lion of London literary society in support of the last of the Stuarts, Queen Anne. When she died in 1714, the tide went out for the likes of Swift, as the long Whig ascendancy – which would last until the 1770s – began.

Suddenly, from being one of the great wits and champions of literary and intellectual London – his preferred and true milieu – he was fobbed off by the new regime with the deanery of St Patrick's Cathedral in Dublin. He might reasonably have expected a bishopric in England had his luck held. But it did not. He was sent into internal exile, back to Ireland. The modern equivalent might have been an ambitious provincial in the old Soviet Union who had backed the wrong horse in the power game being sent off to manage the power station in Omsk.

He hated it. But now his life began. He epitomized the split personality of the Irish Anglican mind, simultaneously resenting English injustice towards Ireland while craving the good opinion of the metropole that was his spiritual home. In this, he stood at the head of a tradition that subsists to the present day. The Irish of every stripe grouse about England while wishing for her good opinion, forgetting that England can hardly give a minute's notice to Ireland and its insular obsessions.

But in Swift's rage and resentment, there was the universal voice of a benevolent, fractured humanity. He was like a damaged teenager in a dysfunctional family, ignored and insulted by those from whom he desired love and to whom he wanted to express love in return. He turned his rage back on England, the father that had rejected him and cast him into exile.

Of English injustice to Ireland there was little doubt. In a mercantilist age, England arranged things to suit herself. There were legal restrictions on Irish trade that damaged Ireland but suited influential English economic interests. Swift's response was *A Proposal for the Universal Use of Irish Manufacture* (1720) urging a boycott of English goods under the memorable rubric that the Irish should 'burn everything English except its coal'.

Next, in the 1720s, came the *Drapier's Letters*. A patent had been granted to a Birmingham ironmaster, William Wood, to manufacture Irish halfpenny coins. It was believed, rightly or wrongly, that Wood got the patent through the influence of one of the king's mistresses. Moreover, he was permitted to produce far more coins than were required, at the risk of inflation in Ireland but at the promise of vast profits for Wood.

Posing as a humble anonymous drapier, Swift led the charge against this patent in a series of six excoriating masterpieces of satire. The true authorship was soon known: Dublin, then as now, was a small city and you couldn't keep a secret for more than about ten minutes. But the *Drapier's Letters* did the trick. Wood's patent was withdrawn and the scheme failed.

What followed were Swift's two masterpieces. The first, *Gulliver's Travels*, was published in 1726. It is an allegorical account of a traveller from civilized Europe to remote, fictional lands. In it, Swift tests the supposed values of civilization against the usages of 'savages'. This is the era in which Europeans are bumping up against previously unknown cultures on the American frontier, in Asia and South America; in which Captain Cook was soon to circumnavigate the globe and discover the exotic South Sea Islands. By presenting the 'other', the unknown or half-known, as more civilized and tolerant than civilized Europeans, Swift turns his misanthropy on his own world.

The second masterpiece was *A Modest Proposal*. Disgusted by the poverty of Ireland, Swift employs his satire to put forward a solution: eat the children of the poor. He rejects all objections to this infant cannibalism on humanitarian grounds, proposing instead the reign of practical necessity. 'I have been assured by a very knowing American of my acquaintance in London that, a young healthy child well nursed is at a year a most delicious, nourishing and wholesome food, whether stewed, roasted, baked or boiled; and I make no doubt that it will equally serve in a fricassee or a ragout.'

There is nothing like it in all of English satire, an invitation to satisfy poverty and hunger by murdering and cannibalizing the children of the poor. There is a sadness in Swift, a sense of existential disappointment behind all the transgressive hilarity: it goes back to his exile in his homeland. If ever a literary genius was driven by his conflicted opposites, it was he.

By the time *A Modest Proposal* was published, Stella was dead. So was Vanessa, the other great love of his life. Her real name was Esther Vanhomrigh, the daughter of the Lord Mayor of Dublin. She fell in love with Swift, whom she had met in London, and followed him back to Dublin when he became dean of St Patrick's. The following years were tense because of his continuing and ambiguous relationship with Stella but there is little doubt of his love – in his own crooked and faltering way – for these two remarkable women.

After their deaths, all was autumnal. Swift suffered a progressive mental decline. As he put it, a tree rots from the top. He died in 1745, leaving much of his fortune for the foundation of a mental hospital that still stands, St Patrick's, noting with one last witty shaft that

He left the little wealth he had
To build a house for fools and mad
And showed with one satiric touch
No nation wanted it so much.

DUKE OF WELLINGTON

The cat born in the stable was the supreme example of the Irishman as provincial made good. His family name was Arthur Wellesley, a poshed-up version of Wesley, which is how the family used to style themselves before they got notions. The Wesleys were of Old English, Hiberno-Norman stock, not Cromwellian, and they were major landowners on the rich pastureland of Co. Meath, north-west of Dublin. But they had long since conformed to the Established Church and were indistinguishable from any other branch of the late eighteenth-century Anglican ascendancy.

Wellington was born in Dublin in 1769, in Merrion Street in the heart of what was then the brand-new Georgian city. The house in which he was born is now part of one of Dublin's most luxurious five-star hotels. His early education was in Ireland but in due course he was sent to Eton where, like many a distinguished person before and since, he did not shine. After a short period in provincial France, during which time he acquired proficiency in French manners and the French language, he enlisted in the British Army.

From 1793 until 1815, Great Britain was at war with Revolutionary and Napoleonic France more or less all the time. Initially, Wellington was remote from the centre of action. He spent a few years as an MP in the Irish House of Commons but his career really took off in India, where he was appointed military secretary to his brother Richard who was the governor of Bengal. It was nepotistic but it worked, as Wellington established his military credentials by reforms in the Indian army that he forced through and by his decisive victory over the forces of Tipu Sultan of Mysore. He was now regarded as a coming man.

Back in Britain, he was appointed Chief Secretary of Ireland, a new office established under the terms of the Act of Union (1801). The Chief Secretary was the representative of the London government in

Dublin, as the Lord Lieutenant or Viceroy was the representative of the crown. His civilian and political responsibilities ran in parallel with his continued military service, although by 1805 the position of the various allied coalitions mustered against Napoleon seemed hopeless. In December 1805, Bonaparte won the Battle of the Three Emperors at Austerlitz and bestrode the continent.

The tide turned in 1809, and Wellington was material to its turning. A guerrilla revolt against French rule in the Iberian Peninsula set off the Peninsular War. Wellington became commander of British troops sent in support of the rebels. He drove the French out of Portugal and eventually across the Pyrenees and out of Spain as well.

The hubristic folly of Napoleon's invasion of Russia in 1812, followed by the French army's horrifying retreat, finally hollowed out Bonaparte's power base. He abdicated, went into exile and then returned, facing the sixth coalition gathered against him – he had defeated the first five – at Waterloo on 18 June 1815. Wellington commanded the allied troops and won – but only just. Left to himself, he would almost certainly have lost. But late in the day, Prussian reinforcements under Blücher proved decisive. It was, as Wellington acknowledged, 'the nearest run thing you ever saw in your life'.

Wellington was now celebrated as 'le vainquer du vainquer du monde', the conqueror of the conqueror of the world. He was 45 years old, incidentally the same age as Napoleon. After this supreme moment, everything that followed in his long life seems like a diminuendo. He became a Tory politician of the most reactionary stripe, opposing both Catholic Emancipation and the Reform Act of 1832, both losing causes. His marriage to Kitty Pakenham, daughter of Lord Longford, was unhappy and he was a serial adulterer and philanderer; this in an age when such activities were regarded tolerantly (how unlike the lives of our contemporary upper classes, with the tabloids sniffing scandal everywhere).

Still, he gave a phrase to the language. He was, along with many others of his class, a client of Harriette Wilson, the most expensive and fashionable courtesan of her day. When her day and her looks began to fade, La Wilson resolved to cash in her chips by writing a memoir in which she proposed to spill the beans on all her clients unless they paid her off. Wellington, well acquainted with her bed, refused with the memorable words: 'Publish, and be damned.'

The Great Exhibition of 1851 opened in the year before Wellington died. It was, in effect, the first World's Fair, in which the inventive achievements of the early Victorian empire were put on display. The exhibition was housed in a vast glasshouse in Hyde Park designed by Joseph Paxton and known as the Crystal Palace. There was just one snag. The upper reaches of the structure were infested by sparrows. The organizers were at a loss as to how to deal with them. There were too many of them and they were too high up. You couldn't shoot them because the bullets would shatter the glass panels. So they called the Duke, to see if he could suggest anything. He surveyed the scene and simply said, 'Sparrowhawks'. And so it was done: *le vainquer du vainquer du monde.*

BRENDAN BRACKEN

Of all the people to make it to the top of English society, Bracken must be one of the most improbable. He was born in 1901 in Co. Tipperary, the second son of J.K. Bracken, one of the seven men who had founded the Gaelic Athletic Association (GAA) in 1884. The GAA was fiercely nationalist in its politics. It is fair to say that Brendan Bracken inherited the ferocity, if not the politics.

The family moved to Dublin and he attended schools there, as well as a Jesuit establishment in Limerick. He was an unruly youth. At a mere 14 years of age, he ran away to Australia, passing himself off in various guises. He returned briefly to Ireland before moving to England, teaching in a number of schools and claiming identities and connections that he did not possess. He bluffed his way through by sheer chutzpah and force of personality.

In 1922 – still only 21 – he moved to London and established himself in the publishing world. Before long, he got an introduction to Winston Churchill, to whom he remained attached for the rest of his life. Churchill's wife considered Bracken a chancer – she was not wrong about that – but he was a resourceful and energetic chancer. By the end of the 1920s, he was the proprietor of a number of magazines and journals – including half-ownership of *The Economist* – a socialite and a Conservative MP. He had a town house in Westminster and a chauffeur-driven car. He was not yet 30.

Ambitious though he obviously was, he remained devoted to Churchill all through the 1930s when it seemed that the older man was a busted flush. But when the war came in 1939, Churchill became First Lord of the Admiralty and Bracken became his parliamentary private secretary, maintaining that role when Churchill moved to 10 Downing Street in May 1940. He also became a privy counsellor. In 1941, he joined the government as Minister for Information, in which role he was generally judged a success. Immediately after the war, he briefly became a cabinet minister as First Lord – Churchill's old job – but his formal political career ended shortly afterwards with the Labour landslide of 1945. He himself lost his seat.

He acquired a peerage, although never took his seat in the House of Lords. He devoted himself to his business interests, which by now included ownership of the *Financial Times*. He was a trustee of the National Gallery, in which capacity he objected strongly to the proposed return of some priceless Impressionist paintings from the Gallery to Dublin, the home intended for them by their owner, the connoisseur Sir Hugh Lane, who had lost his life on board the *Lusitania* in 1915. But the codicil in Lane's will gifting the paintings to Dublin was unsigned and on this quibble Bracken took his stand. He was not alone.

Once he had established himself in Britain in his twenties, he showed scant regard for Ireland, other than his immediate family. He was entirely focused on England and on his business interests and social connections. He died young, of cancer, aged 57. His mentor Churchill survived him by almost a decade.

THE BROADCASTERS
Terry Wogan was already a well-known radio and TV personality in Ireland before he moved to the UK in the late 1960s. Born and educated in Limerick, he was just 30 when he crossed the water. From the 1970s onwards, on both radio and TV, he became one

of the best-loved broadcasters in the country. At one point he was hosting an evening chat show on BBC TV three times a week while his morning radio programme on BBC Radio 2 was reckoned to have the biggest audience of any show in Europe. For many years, he presented the Eurovision Song Contest for the BBC, lampooning its excesses and musical shortcomings with a gentle but telling wit.

His success was all the more improbable because it coincided with a sporadic series of bomb attacks on mainland Britain by the IRA. Sir Terry, as he eventually became, was a reassuring Irish accent, unaffected, charming and witty. He was not the only Irish person to become a media success in Britain at that time but he was by far the most popular.

Gloria Hunniford, like Wogan, had an established media career in Ireland before making her way over the water. She has appeared in numerous TV shows over many years but her most consistent success came from her own radio programme on BBC Radio 2 which ran from the early 1980s to the mid 1990s.

Henry Kelly began his career as a journalist on the *Irish Times*, reporting from Belfast in the early days of the troubles and publishing a brisk account in book form of the fall of the old Stormont regime in 1972. In 1976 he moved to London but four years later he abandoned political journalism for a TV and radio career, presenting a number of daytime shows. His later career was mostly in radio: he was one of the inaugural presenters on Classic FM in 1992, and has remained associated with the station.

Some Brits Who Made the Crossing the Other Way

Derek Hill (1916–2000) was a distinguished landscape and portrait painter who settled in Co. Donegal and founded the Tory Island school of painting.

Bruce Arnold (1936–) studied at Trinity and stayed on in Ireland, becoming its longest-serving political journalist and an authority on Irish fine art.

Nick Leeson (1967–) became notorious as the derivatives broker whose unauthorized bad trades in Singapore broke Barings Bank. After a few years in a Singapore prison, he settled in Co. Galway and became CEO of the local football club, Galway United.

7
ONE TO TEN

ONE OF OUR OWN

Ireland is and always has been intensely localist. The down-home candidate generally gets the vote, especially if he or she stands in contrast to the smoothie-chops up in Dublin. Some of the most popular TDs (Dáil deputies), consistently pulling huge votes, are those that pay relentless and detailed attention to their constituencies. Statesmen need not apply but a neighbour's child who tends his home patch is always in with a shout. In one instance, a strong suspicion of tax evasion – with a judicial opinion in support of it – was insufficient to disturb a rural TD from his accustomed perch at the top of the poll.

TWO LANDS ON ONE SOIL

For years, the sectarian division in Northern Ireland seemed like an anachronistic freak. There was nothing like it anywhere west of Lebanon. Then came the fall of communism and the break-up of Yugoslavia. Before long, Ulster seemed a lot less odd, as the Balkans erupted. It was a reminder that ethnic and religious polarization can develop anywhere, given the right conditions. Happily, at the time of writing, the situation has been contained. But the mutual suspicions have been damped down, not extinguished.

THREE LEAVES ON THE SHAMROCK

The shamrock, a trefoil diminutive clover, is one of the national emblems of Ireland. It acquired this status from the charming myth about St Patrick converting a pagan sub-king to Christianity (see p. 39) by showing him a shamrock to illustrate the Trinitarian nature of the Christian God. Just as the shamrock is a single plant with three leaves, so God is three persons in one. The fact that we have no evidence for this yarn is neither here nor there; nor do we know when it was first put about. The point is that everyone loves a clever story; it's easy to remember; and it makes the national saint out to have been a nifty thinker. That'll do.

FOUR COURTS

This great classical building on the Dublin quays takes its name from the four divisions of medieval common law: the courts of Common Pleas, Exchequer, Chancery and King's Bench. They dealt with, respectively, minor cases, financial cases, equity and serious criminal matters. Various nineteenth-century reforms folded these traditional divisions into the modern courts system. Although Ireland follows English common law, there are customary differences. For instance, barristers are not grouped in chambers, as in London. Instead they foregather in a single large room, the Law Library. By custom, any barrister, no matter how senior, must drop whatever he is doing if a younger person asks for advice or opinion. The Four Courts was badly damaged in the short Irish civil war of 1922–23 but has subsequently been rebuilt.

FIVE POINTS

Ireland has had a dismal record of emigration, especially following the disastrous Great Famine of 1845–52. The United States was the preferred destination but the Irish arrived in New York wretchedly poor. The early emigrants concentrated in Lower Manhattan, at a street intersection known as the Five Points. It was reckoned to be the worst slum in New York. Its contemporary London equivalent was the St Giles district, another slum notorious for attracting poverty-stricken Irish. But in time, the Irish in America – as in Britain – rose in the world and prospered. Then, in the late twentieth century when the domestic Irish economy took off, Ireland suddenly became a land of immigrants, for all of whom the Polish plumber came to stand as symbol.

SIX COUNTIES

What's in a name? When the island was partitioned in 1920, many nationalists and republicans regarded the new entity of Northern Ireland as illegitimate. This was true not only of northern nationalists trapped in the unionist statelet; it was a sentiment shared by many in the south. The upshot was a firm refusal ever to use the official name of the place. Until the 1980s, government ministers and spokesmen in Dublin habitually referred to it as 'the Six Counties'. A variation on this theme was simply to make a general reference to 'the north of Ireland', a formula also favoured by many northern nationalists. The Six Counties was also the formula insisted upon in the style guide to the *Irish Press* newspaper which was controlled by Éamon de Valera and his family until it collapsed in 1995. Northern unionists retaliated by routinely referring to Northern Ireland simply as Ulster, which it is not. Three of the nine Ulster counties are in the Republic. This silly and childish game of semantic mud-throwing has abated in recent times, in line with the general thaw ushered in by the peace process.

SEVEN DRUNKEN NIGHTS

Traditional folk music has always been popular in Ireland and still is. In the 1960s, however, as society began to modernize, there was both a revival and a change of tone in the presentation of the music. At the elite level, a number of outstanding groups – of whom the Chieftains deservedly became the most celebrated – produced performances and recordings to the highest musical standards. Others introduced instruments, such as balalaikas, which horrified the purists but broadened the musical palette. At the more popular end of things, there was a great resurgence of ballads. These too were often sniffed at by the purists but the ballad surge has continued without interruption. The group that initially drove this revival was the Clancy Brothers and Tommy Makem, all of them decked out in white Aran sweaters: they were enormously popular in America. Close to home, the Dubliners were not merely popular – they had a top 20 hit in Britain with their song 'The Seven Drunken Nights', fronted by the late Ronnie Drew, whose Dublin accent was described by one critic as sounding 'like coke being pushed under a door'. The song, a translation from an Irish-language version, concerns a drunk who comes home each night to find another in his bed, only to be reproached by his wife. She has a succession of ingenious excuses, saying that the other man is not a man at all but some other creature of her invention. Befuddled, the husband is fobbed off. The song was banned on RTÉ, the national broadcaster, for indecency. The Irish language version, which is even saltier, was not.

EIGHT YOUNG MEN IN CITY HALL

The Irish Free State – later to mutate into the Republic of Ireland – was born in chaos. The terms of the Anglo-Irish Treaty that established the new state were disputed by doctrinaire republican purists. The result was civil war, which lasted from June 1922 until April 1923. While the number of casualties has never been established with certainty, it was relatively small as these things go: best estimates lie either side of 1,000 dead. But the material destruction was considerable. A poor country could ill-afford the estimated £30 million worth of damage to buildings and infrastructure or the further £17 million spent directly by the new government in the prosecution of the war. Moreover, it also had to find money for dependants' allowances claims, extra money for a new police force and the prison costs associated with incarcerating an estimated 12,000 republican prisoners. Yet somehow the new state managed. Its hard man, Kevin O'Higgins, who was later assassinated by republicans, described the new government in memorable terms: 'we were simply eight young men in City Hall, standing amidst the ruins of one administration with the foundations of another not yet laid and with wild men screaming through the keyholes'.

NINE GLENS OF ANTRIM

One of the things that surprises people about Northern Ireland is how beautiful it can be. The troubles gave it such a bad name that it was easy to forget how attractive many parts of it are. This is nowhere more true than in Co. Antrim, at the very north-east corner of the island, the county closest to Scotland. Its central geographical feature is a mountain range that runs north–south through the middle of the county, with lowlands falling away to the west towards the county border at the River Bann. On the eastern side, a series of nine dramatic glens drop towards the coast. Until the building of the Antrim Coast Road (see p. 86) the people of the glens were hemmed in on the seaward side and effectively cut off from the rest of the island. This accounts for the distinctive subculture of the glens. It is, for instance, the only northern part of the country where hurling is played with any degree of seriousness. Of the nine, Glenariff is dubbed the 'Queen of the Glens'. It contains a celebrated forest park with a number of fine waterfalls. On the coast road, Cushendall is held to be the capital of the glens. It's an attractive place: small, with a population of about 1,500 people, but it is the centre of the annual summer festival which attracts many visitors to this delightful corner of Ireland. It stands where three of the glens meet – Glenaan, Glenballyemon and Glencorp. As the crow flies, you are nearer to Scotland than to Belfast, which feels like another world.

TEN TEN TWENTY

Despite the modernization of Ireland and its position as the European headquarters of many US-based high-tech and pharmaceutical companies, agriculture is still a very significant economic activity. The climate inclines to pasture rather than tillage: this is especially true in the West, where there is more poor land than in the east. Everyone in Ireland above a certain age remembers incessant advertisements on television for a grassland fertilizer called 10-10-20, which takes its name from the fact that its composition is in the proportion of ten parts nitrogen, ten parts phosphate and twenty parts potash. The cultivation of grassland is central to Irish agriculture and to the food industry that depends upon it. Irish meat and dairy products are widely exported and a cherished reputation for being a 'clean food island' is part of the Irish brand. While agriculture by no means constitutes the largest category of Irish exports – pharmaceuticals are way ahead of everything else – it is the only major economic activity that does not depend on foreign direct investment. Moreover, there is a folk memory among the Irish that maintains a mental association with the land. Ownership of the land of Ireland by the people who worked it was a central demand of nationalism, one whose success in the early twentieth century finally killed off the old landlord system. So, while the farmers drive all the townies mad with what seem like their never-ending grumbles and complaints, they still get a free pass on the back of that sentimental attachment to the land. Mind you, the fact that the farmers have one of the most efficient and influential lobbying groups helps as well. No politician outside the bigger cities can afford to disregard the farmers' vote.

8

Literature and Language

The Irish Language

Sometimes called Gaelic or simply Irish, it is a Celtic language introduced to the island around 300 BC. The Celts swept all before them and Gaelic was established as the universal vernacular by the time Christianity came in the fifth century AD. There are two branches of Celtic languages, each coming from a now lost Ur-Celtic. Linguists distinguish them as P-Celtic and Q-Celtic (see p. 16). The distinction is based on pronunciation. In Welsh, for instance, the word for a head (or headland) is 'pen'. In Irish, it is *ceann*, but it is pronounced with an initial 'q' sound. It is also easy to see how geography facilitated this linguistic division, with a rough north–south divide between the two versions. They are long since mutually incomprehensible. On the other hand, Irish-speakers and Scots Gaelic speakers can understand each other and have little trouble reading each other's language.

Unlike England, where Norman French pushed Anglo-Saxon into the shadows for about four centuries, the Hiberno-Normans never established a linguistic hegemony in Ireland. To the contrary, they absorbed Irish themselves. We have already seen (p. 78) that one of the most celebrated Gaelic poets of the medieval period was the man known as *Gearóid Iarla*, or Gerald the Earl. He was no ordinary earl: he was the Earl of Desmond, no less, one of three great magnate families of Ireland in the Middle Ages.

With the arrival of New English adventurers around the time of Elizabeth I, the English language began to get a foothold. This was especially true of the area around Dublin, the seat of English royal power. That said, Dublin remained largely Irish-speaking until the early nineteenth century. The difference was that it was the language of the poor. English had relentlessly advanced as the language of government, law and commerce. Daniel O'Connell, the father of modern Irish nationalism, was famously indifferent to the fortunes of the older language. He saw English as the medium of modernization: 'I am sufficiently utilitarian not to regret its abandonment... Though the Irish language is connected with many recollections that twine around the hearts of Irishmen, yet the superior utility of the English tongue as the medium of all modern communication is so great that I can witness without a sigh the gradual disuse of Irish.'

Later nationalists, towards the end of the nineteenth century, took the opposite view. The Gaelic revival – which also found expression in English through such poetry as that of Yeats – was a key determinant of the final, successful stage of the Irish nationalist struggle. But by then the damage was done. The catastrophic famine of the mid-century, which O'Connell lived long enough to witness, had dealt a death blow to Irish. It hit hardest in Irish-speaking areas in the West. Despite the exertions of the Gaelic League and the educational policy of independent Irish governments which made Irish a compulsory school subject, Ireland remains overwhelmingly an anglophone country. Despite all that compulsory Irish in schools, many (most?) Irish people are less than proficient in the Grand Old Tongue.

That said, there has been a substantial growth in schools where the medium of instruction is the Irish language. These *Gaelscoileanna* are equipping a new generation of children with an easy proficiency in Irish. The death of the language has been foretold for so long, yet it refuses to lie down and die. There is even a barber shop in central Dublin where you can get your hair cut through the medium (they are bilingual, by the way).

Hiberno-English

In recent decades, the version of English spoken in Ireland has been recognized as a separate dialect of Standard English. Its distinctiveness comes from two sources. One is obviously words and construction borrowed from Irish. The other is distance from the metropole: just as American English is quite different in spelling and idiom from Standard English, something similar obtains in Ireland, although not to the same extent.

Some time ago, I was in Australia, where there are thousands of young Irish people. I was on a train going into central Melbourne and I heard an unmistakable Irish accent talking on a mobile phone. The context soon became clear: a colleague of this young man was enquiring about something that was overdue. 'Sure, I'm after sending it to you,' said Pat. This clearly meant nothing to his interlocutor. So he did what every normal person would do. He repeated himself, only louder: 'I told you, I'm after sending it to you.' This pantomime went on a few more times, with our hero getting more and more agitated at the failure of his Aussie boss to understand simple Hiberno-English.

I'm after sending is a pure borrowing from Gaelic. That is how the past tense is formed in that language and it has been hauled body and bones into Irish-English. Other borrowings from Gaelic include the suffix –een, meaning little. Thus maneen (little man) girleen and boreen. The last of these means a little road and is a direct transliteration from Irish: the word for a road is bóthar (pron. bo-har), so a little road is a bótharín, anglicized to boreen. All those place names beginning with Bally are simply an anglicization of baile (pron. bol-ya), which means a town.

Then there are usages peculiar to Ireland: 'your man' as an all-purpose identifier of an individual. Likewise, there is the use of hoor (not whore) in a similar capacity: there are cute hoors (crafty fellows) and poor hoors (innocents). In Ireland, a child is said to be bold, not naughty. A cupboard is a press. You go shopping for the messages. A yoke can be anything at all: that yoke standing in the corner is useless. It could be anything from an Aga to a fly whisk: you just infer the context, as you do with your man.

If you are doing well, you are on the pig's back. An idiot in London becomes an eejit when he crosses the Irish Sea. In Kerry, a very tall, thin man might be called a long fawsthook, from the Irish word fás, meaning growth. A male fool is an amadhaun; a female fool an ownshock, both straight borrowings from Irish. Likewise flahoolach, to be generous or lavish. If something is especially bad, it can be said to be wojus, a mixture of woeful and odious.

Then there are words that have become rare or archaic in Standard English but are still in common use in Ireland. Oxter is a good example: it means an armpit. It can also be heard in Scotland and in some parts of the north of England; again, distance from the metropole is the key. Similarly, the verb to cog means to cheat in an examination: at best, it is now regarded as slang in Standard English, to the extent that it has any currency at all, but is a perfectly respectable usage in Ireland. A scanger (that g is hard) is a young lout (it's a particularly common word in Cork). T.P. Dolan, the greatest living authority on Hiberno-English, speculates that it may be derived from the archaic English word 'scange', to loaf about.

Pronunciation varies quite a bit. To the foreign ear, working-class accents in Belfast, Dublin and Cork will sound disconcertingly unalike. For a small island, regional variations are very marked. The second person of the Christian trinity is usually invoked as Jaysus, thus giving substance to the acronymic greeting AJH: ah, Jaysus, howaya!

Borrowings from Gaelic are rare in Standard English, which is otherwise promiscuous in importing loan words from the corners of the earth. Why this is so is a mystery. Perhaps those uppity Gaels were a bit too close to home for comfort. But take the title of Compton Mackenzie's novel – later made into a movie – *Whisky Galore*. It's pure Gaelic. Whisky from *uisce beatha* (pron. ish-ka baha, the water of life, cognate with the French *eau de vie*) and Galore from *go leór* (a lot).

A boy is a garsún in Irish, which is almost certainly a loan word from Norman French (*garçon*) but the word is used freely in Hiberno-English. If you are on a spree, you're on the ran-tan-tan. Alternatively, you are on a skite. If something meets with the approval of a Dublin working-class youth, it's rapid (no bourgeois would use the word in a fit). In Ulster, if things are going well they are 'stackin' out', which is sticking out, perhaps an obscure reference to the male erection.

And so it goes on. There are genuine dialect words, mostly Gaelic borrowings or Standard English archaisms, slang which varies by region and by class and other terms and usages that are mysterious. It all adds up to a rich linguistic stew and helps to account for the exceptional Irish achievement in literature. That's where we turn to next.

Scribble, Scribble, Scribble

Ireland can claim to have the oldest continuous literary tradition in Europe. Whether it can make good the claim is another matter – the Welsh have made the same claim. But one way or another, the tradition is long and continuous. Even today, a heroic minority of writers still publish fiction and poetry in Irish. But it is literature in English for which Ireland has achieved pre-eminence in the world of letters in recent centuries.

There have been four Irish winners of the Nobel Prize for Literature. None of them was James Joyce, although he was the greatest writer of them all (see p. 59). In 1938, while Joyce was still alive, the prize went to Pearl S. Buck in what is generally reckoned to be the worst decision in the prize's history. The four Irish winners were W.B. Yeats (see p.56), George Bernard Shaw, Samuel Beckett and Seamus Heaney.

Shaw was born in Dublin in 1856 but lived most of his life in London. He was a force of nature, a major playwright – although the whirligig of fashion has been unkind to him recently – a formidable music critic, a Fabian socialist and a controversialist. He was a notable figure in British public life for most of his adult life. He won the prize in 1925.

By contrast, Beckett was intensely private. Born in Dublin in 1906, he spent most of his life in France and played no public role, although he fought with the French Resistance during the war. He generally wrote in French and translated his own work into English. His play *En Attendant Godot/Waiting for Godot* was first performed in 1953 and can fairly claim to be the most revolutionary drama of the century. It is a study in futility, rich in a comedy of unfulfilled longing. One critic (Irish, wouldn't you know?) described it as a play in which nothing happens, twice. Beckett was also a novelist of the first distinction. His prize was awarded in 1969.

Seamus Heaney was the most recent winner of the prize, in 1995. A poet of exceptional range and curiosity, he employed the rich dialect of the Ulster countryside in his work but his themes ranged far from home. A classicist and critic as well as a poet, he rendered translations of Greek drama as well as a superb version of *Beowulf*, the Anglo-Saxon saga. A courtly man, his death in 2013 was widely mourned.

Some other Irish writers of note, with one favourite work from each. First, dramatists:

Oscar Wilde	*The Importance of Being Earnest*
John M. Synge	*The Playboy of the Western World*
Sean O'Casey	*The Plough and the Stars*
Sebastian Barry	*The Steward of Christendom*

Next, novelists:

John Banville	*The Sea*
Roddy Doyle	*The Commitments*
Colm Toibín	*The Story of the Night*
Anne Enright	*The Gathering*
Emma Donoghue	*Room*
Brendan Behan	*Borstal Boy*
Dermot Healy	*A Goat's Song*
Aidan Higgins	*Langrishe, Go Down*
Somerville & Ross	*The Real Charlotte*
John McGahern	*Amongst Women*
Flann O'Brien	*At Swim-Two-Birds*

Ireland has always been a stronghold of the short story. Among the masters of the form are:

George Moore	Mary Lavin
Frank O'Connor	William Trevor
Sean O'Faolain	

Finally, some poets other than Seamus Heaney:

Derek Mahon	'A Disused Shed in Co. Wexford'
Michael Longley	'Ceasefire'
Brendan Kennelly	'My Dark Fathers'
John Montague	'Like Dolmens Round My Childhood...'
John Hewitt	'An Irishman in Coventry'
Louis MacNeice	'Autumn Journal'
Patrick Kavanagh	'The Great Hunger'
Dorothy Molloy	'Les Grands Seigneurs'

Irish winners of the Man Booker Prize:

Roddy Doyle	*Paddy Clarke Ha Ha Ha*	1993
John Banville	*The Sea*	2005
Anne Enright	*The Gathering*	2007

Irish Murdoch, who won the prize in 1978 for her novel, *The Sea, the Sea*, is sometimes claimed for Ireland. Although she was born in Dublin, her parents moved to London when she was only a few weeks old. Her education, formation and sensibility were completely English.

Four Literary Landscapes

DUBLIN

The capital city of any country is likely to dominate its literature. Dublin is no exception but it owes its centrality to one book above all, Joyce's *Ulysses*. This masterpiece is set in the city and its environs with all the action, much of it inconsequential, taking place on a single day, 16 June 1904.

The sense of place is overwhelming. Some writers have this knack of conveying place and furnishing the reader with a sense of knowing it: Philip Roth's Newark, New Jersey; Carson McCullers' small-town American South; Balzac's Paris; Dickens' London. This ability to conjure up a mental landscape that seems completely unforced and authentic is among the more wondrous accomplishments of a great writer's art.

No one has ever done it better than Joyce. He once said that if the city were destroyed, it could be rebuilt from reading his masterpiece. That's a slight exaggeration – one hopes that it will never have to be tested in real life. He did, however, take the trouble in exile to memorize the name of every shop in a number of given streets, in the correct sequence, as of 1904 in order to achieve the greatest possible realism. When he was unsure, he wrote home to his relations to check.

It is precisely the realism of the book that makes it so compelling. Behind all the worries about its obscurities and difficulties, its rambling self-indulgence – no editor ever got next or near the text – and its sheer verbal exuberance, it is that realism, that rendering of the city of Dublin on the page with a fidelity that is uncanny, that defines the Irish capital as a literary landscape.

In more recent times, Roddy Doyle has set his work not simply in Dublin but in parts of the city that are not the standard locales for fiction. His early work, in particular, is set among the working-class suburban estates of the northside, the less fashionable side of the city. O'Casey wrote of the slums in the early twentieth century – no one did it better – but these were city centre slums. The same is true of James Plunkett's superb novel, Strumpet City. Until Doyle, hardly anyone of note had written about the forgotten housing estates in the least attractive corners of town.

Prior to Doyle, literary Dublin meant bourgeois Dublin with a dash of bohemia thrown in for good measure. This was the world of Oliver St John Gogarty, surgeon and wit, so cruelly lampooned by Joyce in Ulysses as the vulgarian Buck Mulligan. It was the world of George Moore, a writer who also felt the lash of Joyce's pen, when he referred to one of Moore's works as having been 'written by Moore, a genuine gent / that lives on his property's ten per cent' (Moore was independently wealthy, being a substantial landowner in the West of Ireland). It was even the exigent world of Patrick Kavanagh, the finest Irish poet between Yeats and Heaney.

Louis MacNeice, not himself a Dubliner and a poet with an

ambiguously jaundiced view of Ireland, caught the city as well as anyone other than Joyce: 'Grey brick upon brick, / declamatory bronze / on sombre pedestals– / O'Connell, Grattan, Moore– / and the brewery tugs and the swans / on the balustraded stream / and the bare bones of a fanlight /over a hungry door / and the air soft on the cheek / and porter running from the taps / with a head of yellow cream / and Nelson on his pillar / watching his world collapse.' Perhaps it took a Belfast man to see Dublin with such clarity at the mid century.

Slieve Luachra

This is an area in the eastern part of Co. Kerry, centred on the town of Castleisland, which has maintained a remarkable musical and literary tradition. It was the birthplace of two of the greatest Irish-language poets of the eighteenth century – indeed, two of the last in a long and noble tradition, as Ireland proceeded to anglicize from the nineteenth century onwards.

They were Egan O'Rahilly, whom we have already encountered (see p. 78) and – from the latter part of the century – Eoghan Rua Ó Súilleabháin, or in English Owen Roe O'Sullivan. O'Sullivan was celebrated contemporaneously as 'Owen of the sweet mouth' and his poetry is full of technical virtuosity. But he was poor, scratching a living as an occasional teacher and a casual labourer. He even spent some time in the Royal Navy on board HMS *Formidable* and wrote a poem, 'Rodney's Glory' in English to celebrate his admiral's victory over the French in a naval engagement in 1782.

O'Sullivan's rackety life was almost a parody of a poet's imagined existence. But his verse has survived, much of it set to music and passed down the generations by oral as well as written tradition.

It is no accident that Slieve Luachra was and remains a strong centre of traditional music. Some of its most revered modern practitioners hail from the area. It was also the birthplace of Fr Patrick Dinneen (1860–1934), best remembered for his idiosyncratic *Irish–English Dictionary* (1927), which drew the repeated withering scorn of Flann O'Brien, writing in the *Irish Times* under the name Myles na gCopaleen. Dinneen was also the author of the first novel in Irish ever published in book form (1901).

Not far from Slieve Luachra, in north Kerry, lies the town of Listowel which has also produced a number of fine writers: the poet Brendan Kennelly, the playwright John B. Keane, the novelist Maurice Walsh and the short story writer Bryan MacMahon.

The Great Blasket

This is the most extraordinary and improbable location of all. It is a large island, just off the coast of the Dingle Peninsula in West Kerry. The tiny coast road hugs the southern end of the peninsula until it reaches Slea Head, where it turns north. And there it is, just across the Blasket Sound, the big island looking for all the world like a crouched lion. It is very beautiful.

Until 1953, the island was inhabited, although at no time since the Famine were there more than 200 inhabitants. It was primitive, with only a little agriculture possible – and very basic at that. Fishing was the principal means of subsistence. Supplies had to be fetched from the mainland across Blasket Sound. There was no church: once again, people had to cross to the mainland for their religious observances.

It was the least promising community one could imagine to be the source of exceptional literature. Yet the Great Blasket produced three memoirs of real merit. The least of them, and for a time the most famous, was by Peig Sayers (1873–1958). It was an oral memoir, dictated to one of her sons in her old age, and in Irish titled *My Own Story*. The work attracted the admiration of ethnologists, folklorists and critics alike. Its series of narrative tales – some of them tall – enthralled a generation for whom the simplicities of the western peasant life represented a special kind of Irish authenticity. A later reaction against the work arose partly from the fact that its ubiquitous presence in the school system associated it with the resentment many urban dwellers showed to the government policy of compulsory Irish.

The most substantial of the three memoirs was the work of Tomás Ó Criomthainn (1854–1937). First published in Irish in 1929, it was translated into English by the Oxford scholar Robin Flower and issued as The Islandman in 1937. It was instantly recognized as a classic. It combines autobiography, sociology and the most complete description of island life that we possess. Ó Criomthainn was a remarkable person: illiterate until about the age of 40, he learned to write and unlocked his native intelligence and linguistic dexterity. As an account of a tiny pre-industrial society on the margins of the world, The Islandman is hard to beat.

The final book to come from this improbable insular landscape was Muiris Ó Súilleabháin's Fiche Bliain ag Fás, better known under its English-language title, Twenty Years A-Growing. Ó Súilleabháin (O'Sullivan) joined the Gardaí (police) and was posted to Connemara, a Gaeltacht area in Co. Galway. It was there that he wrote the book that secured his fame. Like Tomás Ó Criomthainn, he was fortunate to have the patronage and support of an English scholar, George Thomson. Twenty Years A-Growing was published in 1933 – prior to the English-language publication of The Islandman. Ó Súilleabháin was a generation younger than Ó Criomthainn – his dates were 1904–50 – and his perspective varied accordingly. The book was translated into a number of languages. He retired from the Gardaí and wrote a sequel as well as practising magazine journalism. He drowned while swimming off the coast of Co. Galway.

The Blasket islands occupy a unique place in Irish memory and imagination. The tiny Irish-speaking population was removed to the mainland in 1953, the government feeling that it could no longer afford to offer the state's protection to such a remote and storm-lashed outpost. The fame of the island rests on the survival of this primitive fishing community for so long into the modern era. But the memory of that survival depended entirely upon the publication of these three books, written by islanders themselves in the last days of human habitation.

The Golden Vale

Co. Tipperary is as different to the Blasket islands as any two landscapes in the same country could be. Rich, rolling limestone pastureland, this was part of the great medieval earldom of Desmond. In the eighteenth century, it was a hotbed of Whiteboy activities. The Whiteboys were an agrarian protest movement that did not scruple to use violence to oppose land enclosure and other modernizing schemes that benefited landlords but compromised the traditional 'moral economy' whereby mutual social obligations and protections crossed class lines and afforded a degree of security to the less advantaged. An English analogue for the Whiteboys and other Irish agrarian groups was the Captain Swing riots of 1830, prompted by similar circumstances.

As a literary landscape, the Golden Vale depends overwhelmingly on one book. That is *Knocknagow* by Charles Kickham. Published in 1879, it was subtitled 'The Homes of Tipperary'. Kickham had been born in 1828 in the village of Mullinahone in the east of the county, the son of a well-to-do shopkeeper. He became a Fenian, a land agitator and a strong supporter of the tenant farmers in their campaign to weaken and destroy the landlord system. All this was material to his book.

The book is sentimental, melodramatic and not particularly well written. But it caught the moment. The representation of the Kearney family as upstanding tenant farmers at the whim of a callous landlord system spoke to contemporary Ireland like nothing else. In these tenants, virtue was invested. They stood for community solidarity, decency, courage. While the characterization was simplistic, Kickham's principal aim was political, not literary. The condescension of later critics would hardly have troubled him; it certainly did not deter his thousands of readers. The book is still available commercially.

There are many fine characterizations in the book, the most famous of which concerns one Matt the Thresher. He is engaged in a hammer throwing competition with the Captain, a local landlord. Matt allows that the Captain is a decent man and in the ordinary way of things he would be content to lose the contest honourably. But as he lines up his throw, Matt sees in the distance the houses and cabins of the local village and he resolves to win 'for the honour of the little village'. He duly wins with a record throw.

The symbolism is not exactly subtle but it had a galvanizing effect on generations of Irish people. Published as it was on the eve of the land war, the obvious representation of Matt and the Kearneys as the repository of human decency struck a deep chord, how deep may be judged from the fact that it went through numerous editions – probably one a year until well into the twentieth century. It became *the* book by which nationalist Ireland measured its own symbolic virtue. It furnished a myth for a nation.

9
FOOD AND DRINK

In an earlier chapter (see pp. 7–8), I gave a list of favourite beauty spots and beaches based on personal preference. At this point, I think it reasonable to address the important question of food and drink with opinions more widely canvassed from others, to offer a more comprehensive consensus on what's best about eating and drinking in Ireland. Let's start with that quintessential Irish institution, the public house.

Pubs – Central Dublin

We'll ramble around the country, county by county, but it's best to start in the capital. Maybe it's the people I asked to make suggestions, but there is a definite bias in this list towards the more traditional, Victorian boozers. I've tried to compensate by including some more modern, cool places – although few people desire to be cool less than me.

THE PALACE BAR
At 21 Fleet Street, at the top of Temple Bar, just off Westmoreland Street. There has been a pub here since 1823, although the claim that the present building dates from then seems doubtful to my eye. The place has all the characteristics of a mid-Victorian gin palace. It's a style unlikely to have been embraced in Dublin as early as the 1820s; the nineteenth-century city was conservative architecturally and vestiges of the glorious Georgian past lingered until as late as 1860. No matter: this is a superb establishment, with a short narrow bar that opens out into the famous back room.

The room's fame derives from the 1940s, when it was the centre of Dublin literary life, a meeting place for writers and wits of every sort. The presiding genius was R.M. (Bertie) Smyllie, the editor of the *Irish Times* from 1934 to 1954, a man who weighed more than 20 stone, had the small fingernail of his left hand pared in the shape of a nib, like Keats, and cycled around Dublin wearing a sombrero. In a city that loves characters, he was the real thing. He was also an editor of genius, nurturing the talents of a brilliant editorial team, not the least of whom was Flann O'Brien, who wrote a thrice-weekly column under the pseudonym (double pseudonym, actually, because Flann O'Brien was itself one: his real name was Brian O'Nolan) Myles na Gopaleen.

The Bank
At 20 College Green, this red sandstone building built in an Ulster-derived Scots baronial style – most uncommon in Dublin – was originally a busy branch of the Royal Bank of Ireland, long since subsumed into Allied Irish Banks. It was originally built as the Dublin office of the then Belfast Bank: ergo the style.

The bar is the old banking hall and for sheer visual exuberance, there is nothing to touch it in Dublin. Those old bankers threw money at their principal buildings, generating confidence in the soundness of their institutions with architectural display. This has all been preserved and enhanced. Downstairs, in what were the original bank vaults, the great safes still stand.

The Old Stand
There has been a public house on the corner of Andrew Street and Exchequer Street for centuries but this building is at the modern end of traditional. It has a cosy, bourgeois feel to it. Indeed, it has a long association with the rugby community, rugby being the bourgeois game par excellence. Decent if unexceptional food and friendly staff.

The International Bar
Just across from the Old Stand, on the other corner of Andrew Street, the one with Wicklow Street, stands the International, a small bar with a lovely Victorian interior. In more recent times, its upstairs room has become one of the leading comedy venues in town. It also hosts jazz and other music events.

PETER'S PUB

At the top of South William Street, where it becomes Johnson Place, Peter's Pub is a haven of quiet. There is no TV (well, there is, but it's only on for an exceptional sports event), and none of the raucousness that you can find in certain pubs. There is almost a monastic feel to Peter's, devoted as it is to the two things that a pub should encourage: drink and conversation.

THE LONG HALL

In South Great George's Street, this has a claim to be the loveliest Victorian pub in Dublin. Like the Palace, it has a rectangular bar that opens into a wider back room. But what dazzles are the mirrors, the bric-a-brac, the visual chutzpah of the place. Not as grand as the Bank but just as impressive.

THE LIBRARY BAR

Around the corner from the Long Hall, on Exchequer Street, stands the Central Hotel. Normally, hotel bars are pretty nondescript. Not this first-floor beauty. It is decked out like a club library, with generous armchairs and bookcases around the walls. Ah, books do furnish a room.

THE STAG'S HEAD

Leave the Library Bar, turn left and immediately left again and at the end of Dame Court you'll find the Stag's Head. The wonderful Victorian bar is dominated by a huge – you guessed it – stag's head. There is a sort of glorified snug in at the back, actually a small lounge. Like every pub mentioned in this list, it's somebody's favourite.

NEARY'S

On Chatham Street, just off Grafton Street, Neary's is instantly recognizable by the two lamps outside the door supported by two brackets in the shape of human arms, both excellent pieces of craftsmanship. Within, the clubbiest pub in the city. Again, like Peter's nearby, there is no music or TV. Neary's has a long theatrical association: its rear door opens on to a laneway, on the other side of which is the stage door of the Gaiety Theatre.

DAVY BYRNE'S
Joyce's 'moral pub' in Duke Street, where half of the eighth episode of *Ulysses* is set. Mr Bloom, having tried the Burton across the street for lunch (now the Bailey pub), but disgusted by the coarse eating habits of the diners, retreats to the quieter pub over the way. There, he meets one of the book's minor comic characters, Nosey Flynn, so-called because of a permanent dewdrop on the end of his nose which he snuffles up just in time. Don't go to Davy Byrne's expecting to see what Bloom saw. The pub was rebuilt in the 1940s in a cocktail-bar, art deco style. It's lovely. Every 16 June, Joyceans foregather here in full Edwardian fig to celebrate the day and have the lunch that Bloom had: a Gorgonzola sandwich and a glass of burgundy (just the one?).

KEHOE'S
At 9 South Anne Street this classic late Victorian watering hole describes itself as one of the best-kept secrets in the city centre. I'd say it is one of the worst kept. It's never short of custom, which even spills out on to the street at times. You'll see why it's so popular.

THE DAWSON LOUNGE
The smallest pub in Dublin, located in a basement. You could walk past it six times and miss it every time. Don't: it's a gem. But you'll have to find it first. Hint: it's towards the top of Dawson St, more or less opposite the Mansion House, on the right-hand side going up towards St Stephen's Green.

THE SHELBOURNE BAR
Dublin posh – and another proof that not all hotel bars are indifferent places. On St Stephen's Green North, the Shelbourne is a Dublin institution. The bar is big, generous and roomy. A smaller bar, called the Horseshoe, is on the other side of reception.

DOHENY & NESBITT

In Baggot Street Lower we are back in full Victorian mode, except for the more modern, and less successful, big room at the end of bar. It's the bar itself or one of the snugs that you want to make for. D&N became a household name in the 1980s when, during yet another economic crisis, a group of journalists, economists, civil servants from nearby Government Buildings and even the odd politician prescribed the medicines needed to cure old Ireland's ills. They became known collectively as the Doheny & Nesbitt school of economics.

TONER'S

Toner's is just across the street from D&N and is set out in a similar style, although without any unfortunate back room. For that reason, many consider it the superior pub but both places have their partisans – and both deserve them.

MATT THE THRESHER

Named for the hero of *Knocknagow* (see p. 138) this modern gastropub does some of the best food in any city pub. Its fish is outstanding, well up to if not superior to restaurant standard. But equally, if you just want a pint, there's a place for you here as well.

MULLIGAN'S

It's been trading here in Poolbeg Street since 1782. There is nothing grand about it, but if you like your pubs shabby and authentic, you'll like it a lot.

In the Suburbs

This is a simple listing of some pubs of character and note in the suburbs.

Finnegan's of Dalkey, near the DART station, forever associated with the author Maeve Binchy.

Ashtons of Clonskeagh, down by the Dodder river.

Harry Byrne's on the Howth Road at Clontarf has no sign to indicate it's a pub.

The Hole in the Wall, Blackhorse Avenue, a twee establishment right beside the Phoenix Park.

Jack O'Rourke's, an ornate pub in the centre of Blackrock.

The Gravediggers (otherwise Kavanagh's), Prospect Square, Glasnevin: hidden away but worth the search.

The Other Cities

BELFAST

The Crown Liquor Saloon at 46 Victoria Street. This is the ultimate gin palace. It's owned by the UK National Trust and its ornate interior almost defies description. Exuberant isn't in it. It is right across the street from the Europa Hotel which heroically survived being the most bombed hotel in Europe during the troubles. But the Crown Bar really is a treasure.

The Duke of York, 7–11 Commercial Court. It's down an alleyway. In Belfast they are called entries, just as in Yorkshire they are called snickets. Old fashioned and fun, handily in the city centre.

The John Hewitt is at 51 Donegall Street, near St Anne's Cathedral. A well-mannered, traditional bar. Named in memory of a fine poet and scholar and all-round good man, it occupies what were once the printing offices of the *Belfast News-Letter* and is unusual in being owned by a charity, the Belfast Unemployed Resource Centre.

Kelly's Cellars, 30–32 Bank Street, another city centre gem, with excellent food and lots of music. Very popular.

Cork

Moving to the far end of the island, we won't be thirsty here for long. By general agreement, these are not all the good pubs in the southern capital but there are few who will dispute that these are among the very best.

Dan Lowery's Tavern, 13 MacCurtain Street, Cork. A small, long-established and attractive bar, handy for the nearby Metropole Hotel and the railway station.

The Bodega at St Peter's Market, Cornmarket Street. If there was a competition to find the most beautiful bar in Ireland, the Bodega would surely make the shortlist – and who knows, might even go all the way. A grande dame.

The Oval, South Main Street, is architecturally and decoratively curious in a Cork context. The reason is simple. It was designed by an Edinburgh architect commissioned by the local Beamish & Crawford brewery. The Scots modernist influence is palpable.

The Mutton Lane Inn, 3 Mutton Lane, a long-established and much-loved bar just off Patrick Street in the city centre.

Sin É, 8 Coburg Street, is probably the best of all Cork pubs for traditional music, with a tradition going back to the late nineteenth century. The name is Irish for 'that's that' or perhaps 'it's all over', an ironic reference to the undertaker's premises next door. It's pronounced Shin-eh.

Galway

Although Galway is an anglophone city, it's very conscious of the Connemara Gaeltacht immediately to the west. You'll hear more Irish spoken here than in most Irish cities. Moreover, the town is full of music, so there is no need to mention the availability of musical sessions in the context of a given pub. You will find music all over the place.

Tigh Neachtain, 17 Cross Street, is probably the best-known and most visible pub in town, being right on the main tourist drag. Lots of nooks and snugs.

The Crane Bar, 2 Sea Road. 'Authentic' is the word most commonly associated with this bar. It's small and much loved by locals and visitors alike.

Róisín Dubh, 9 Dominick Street Upper, is yet another music pub but it has a more varied and eclectic repertoire than most. It's also a good stand-up comedy venue.

Tig Cóilí on Mainguard Street, which is just off Shop Street and near St Nicholas' Collegiate Church, is another popular venue.

The point about Galway is that the centre is very compact; small, if you prefer. All these premises are within easy strolling distance of each other and there are dozens more that could have been listed had space allowed.

LIMERICK

The city has often had a bad press because of high rates of violent crime in some areas. But the centre is a Georgian gem, laid out in the late eighteenth century on a rational grid pattern. It is second only to Georgian Dublin in architectural distinction. It also has some fine pubs. Here are a few of them.

Charlie St George, 41–43 Parnell Street, has been a Limerick stalwart since 1883, situated across from the railway station.

Nancy Blake's, 19 Upper Denmark Street, is cosy with a beer garden at the rear. Another one of those pubs where conversation is king, although there are music sessions as well.

Flannery's, 17 Upper Denmark Street, is next door to Nancy Blake's. It is one of the most traditional bars in the city, with a deserved reputation for stocking a huge range of whiskeys.

Tom Collins Pub, 34 Cecil Street. Just another beautiful bar.

Around the Country

This listing excludes the cities already listed. It can't possibly be comprehensive. It is a distilled listing informed by the enthusiasm, bias, prejudice and love of about twenty people who are in a position to know. In most instances, the lists are given without comment. Where the odd comment is added, you can be sure that we are referring to an exceptional establishment.

Co. Wicklow
Glenmalure Lodge, in the deep heart of the Wicklow Mountains.
Mac's Bar, Enniskerry.
Jack White's Inn, long a landmark on the old road south towards Arklow and Wexford.

Co. Wexford
Mary Barry's Bar, Kilmore.
The Coach House, Gorey.
The Sky and the Ground, 112 South Main Street, Wexford.

Co. Waterford
Jack Meade's, on the Passage East road just east of Waterford city.
Geoff's, 9 John Street, Waterford.
The Gingerman Bar, 6 Arundel Lane, Waterford.

Co. Cork (excluding the city)
Murph's Tavern at East Ferry, a little out of the way but worth it.
Aherne's Seafood Bar in Youghal is really part of a fine hotel: excellent.
Bushe's Bar, The Square, Baltimore.
O'Sullivan's Bar, Crookhaven.
Barleycove Beach Hotel, Mizen Head, the most southerly point in Ireland.

Dintys, Union Hall.
    Glandore Inn, Glandore.

Co. Kerry

South Pole Inn, Anascaul, on the road from Tralee to Dingle. Named for the Antarctic explorer Tom Crean, who was a former owner.
John Benny's Pub, Dingle.
The Blue Bull, Sneem.
Kruger's, Dunquin, the most westerly pub in Europe.

Co. Limerick

Aunty Lena's, Adare.

Co. Clare

Monks, Ballyvaughan.
Bofey Quinn's, Corofin.
Cooley's House, Ennistymon.
Crotty's, Market Square, Kilrush.
Durty Nelly's, Bunratty.
Fawl's, O'Connell St, Ennis.

Co. Galway

Moran's of the Weir, Kilcolgan. Deservedly famous for oysters and seafood.
Breathnach's, Oughterard.
Connolly's, Kinvara.
Donnelly's, Barna.
E.J. King's, Clifden.
Molly's Bar, Letterfrack.

Co. Mayo

Matt Molloy's, Westport.
Pat Cohan's Bar, Cong.
Bar One, Castlebar.
The Broken Jug, Ballina.

Co. Donegal
Smuggler's Creek, Rossnowlagh.
Brennan's, Bundoran.
Nancy's, Ardara.

That covers the most popular tourist counties. Here is a selection from the other counties:

Kyteler's Inn, Kilkenny.
Ging's Bar, Carrick-on-Shannon, Co. Leitrim.
Sean's Bar, Athlone, Co. Westmeath. Claims to be the oldest pub in Ireland.
Fitzpatrick's, on the road from Dundalk to Carlingford, Co. Louth. Best chowder east of Boston.
Hargadon's, Sligo, outstanding traditional bar in town centre.
Morrissey's, Abbeyleix, Co. Laois. One half bar, one half grocer's shop. Wonderful.

Restaurants

After liquids, solids. Some of the pubs mentioned above serve excellent food but overall the food culture in Ireland, while improving yearly, is a mile wide and an inch deep. There is no tradition of *cuisine paysanne* such as you find in France or Italy. But there are some foods and dishes that are either unique to Ireland or that are as good here as anywhere.

IRISH STEW
The national dish, based on mutton, onions and potatoes. Latterly, other ingredients have been added, to the dismay of traditionalists and purists. These include carrots, celery and turnips, not to mention various herbs. These additions, in all truth, augment a basic dish that can be rather too plain for the modern palate. Irish stew has been recognized as the signature Irish recipe since at least the eighteenth century, with even English balladeers singing its praises:

But the best feed between I and you
Is some mutton with onions and potatoes
Made into a real Irish Stew
That will stick to your belly like glue.

SODA BREAD

There are many variations on this theme and the bread can be white or brown as you choose, but when the result is good, this is bread as good as anything anywhere. The basic ingredients are flour, salt, bread soda and buttermilk. Topped with a lovely crust and slathered with salted butter, it can be enjoyed at any time of day and in any circumstance.

COLCANNON

The association between Ireland and the potato is so well established as to be unshakeable. Colcannon is basically mashed potato mixed with boiled cabbage or kale, with scallions (spring onions) added. Cream, butter and pepper are essential. The result is delicious. In Ulster, a slight variation on the theme produces champ, in which scallions play the major role to the exclusion of cabbage or kale.

BACON AND CABBAGE

A simple, wholesome dish comprising back bacon with cabbage – either York or Savoy – and boiled potatoes. Traditionally it was garnished with white sauce and parsley. It is a distant cousin of the *choucroute garnie* that is a staple dish in Alsace, although the Irish dish is bland on the palate in comparison.

DUBLIN CODDLE

Pork sausages and back rashers boiled up in a stew with potatoes, salt and pepper. It's not to everyone's taste but it was a staple of the Dublin poor. It has made a comeback on some pub menus – generally jazzed up with herbs and spices to give it a lift – but you won't find it on restaurant menus.

BOXTY

Potato cakes. Boiled potatoes, with salt, butter, flour and perhaps some bacon, all mashed and fried. Very simple but very good. Boxty has inspired balladeers:

> Did you ever take potato cakes or boxty to the school?
> Tucked underneath your oxter, with your book and slide
>   and rule,
> and when teacher wasn't looking, a big bite you did take
> Of the creamy, mealy, sweet potato cake.

DRISHEEN

This is a Cork speciality. It is a blood pudding based on beef and sheep by-products generated in the city's many slaughterhouses. As we saw already (p. 80), Cork was the great entrepôt for the export of every kind of meat from the rich pasturelands of Munster. The presence of abattoirs ensured a certain supply of these by-products, thus stimulating their productive and practical use.

CORNED BEEF

Also called salted beef, it too was a critical part of the Irish rural economy in the eighteenth century and after. In 1776, Cork exported 109,052 barrels of salted beef to England, the continent and North America. The advantages of preserved and salted meat in satisfying the soldiers and sailors of the crown in the long series of wars against the French from 1756 to 1815 hardly needs to be elaborated. In modern times, corned beef and cabbage is often employed as a variation on the theme of bacon and cabbage.

BARM BRACK

This is a yeasted loaf with dried fruit – usually raisins and sultanas – through it. It is sweeter than ordinary bread but is not a cake. Barm is the yeast derived from the latter stages of the brewing process, whereas the word brack is probably just a transliteration of the Irish word for speckled, presumably a reference to the fruit. It is eaten sliced and buttered and is the centrepiece of Hallowe'en when, by tradition, a cheap brass ring is embedded in the brack: the person who gets the ring will be the next to marry.

Michelin-starred Restaurants

There are twelve Michelin-starred restaurants in Ireland. None has three stars.

TWO STARS
Restaurant Patrick Guilbaud, Merrion Hotel, Merrion Street, Dublin.

ONE STAR
Chapter One, Parnell Square, Dublin.
L'Ecrivain, Baggot Street, Dublin.
The Greenhouse, Dawson Street, Dublin.
Heron & Grey, Blackrock, Co. Dublin.
Aniar, Lower Dominick Street, Galway.
Loam, Fairgreen Road, Galway.
Cliff House, Ardmore, Co. Waterford.
Campagne, Gas House Lane, Kilkenny.
Lady Helen, Mount Juliet, Thomastown, Co. Kilkenny.
Eipic, Howard Street, Belfast.
Ox, Oxford Street, Belfast.

Beverages

As in England, tea is still the most popular drink. But coffee has increased hugely in popularity in the last twenty years or so and coffee shops are now ubiquitous. In a land with abundant rainfall and no shortage of natural water, it is surprising to find bottled mineral water everywhere. Indeed, some Irish brands have proved to be major commercial successes, helped by the fact that occasional pollution of the mains water supply has made ordinary tap water impotable in some parts of the country. The domestic consumption of wine has likewise increased hugely and off-licences are to be found in most well populated areas and in all supermarkets. This is partly a function of increased continental travel but is also a consequence of the legal ban on smoking in public places – which has hit pubs hard – and of the increased rigour with which the drink-driving laws are policed.

Fish

For an island surrounded by rich fishing grounds, the reluctance of the Irish to eat fish was something of a mystery. It has been speculated that the traditional Roman Catholic prohibition on eating meat on Friday made fish – the obvious alternative – appear to be a penitential food. At any rate, the old prejudice has largely disappeared and fish is now to be found on every menu, in restaurants and pubs alike.

There has always been one huge exception to the reluctance to eat fish. Ireland, as much as England, is a great bastion of fish and chips. This classic fast food, developed in England in the 1860s, soon made its way to Ireland. There, it became associated with a number of southern Italian families all of whom came from an area known as the Val di Comino about 100 km east of Rome. Their descendants are still the backbone of the Irish chipper. Traditionally thought of as a rather rough-and-ready dish, fish and chips has come up in the world in recent years: most pubs that do decent food offer fish and chips. Even some restaurants have followed suit.

There is still a shortage of wet-fish shops where fresh fish can be bought for domestic consumption. They are, perhaps unsurprisingly, concentrated in fishing ports. It is no accident that while the publishing of new cookbooks goes from strength to strength, books that focus exclusively on fish sell in smaller quantities than general cookbooks.

The Irish seafood industry is none the less a significant part of the Irish economy. It employs more than 10,000 people, including fishermen – the largest single category – fish farmers, a developing area that is the source of occasional controversy on environmental grounds, and processors. Significantly, the export market is greater than the domestic market, with France by far the most important overseas destination for Irish fish.

At home, the old prejudice against fish has almost totally disappeared. The cookbook example noted above suggests that many Irish people are still not confident about cooking fish, but there is no reluctance to order it when eating out. The fish most commonly found on Irish menus are these:

> Salmon
> Trout
> Sea bass
> Hake
> Mackerel
> Shellfish: oysters, crab, crayfish, mussels

Cheese

The other food traditionally eschewed by the Irish is cheese, despite the country having conditions ideal for all dairy produce. The tradition of cheese-making in Gaelic Ireland died out in the seventeenth and eighteenth centuries. It has been speculated that the transfers of land ownership, combined with the rise of the lucrative butter trade, were factors contributing to this decline.

Happily, the situation has been reversed in quite dramatic style since the 1970s. Ireland now produces world-class cheeses, which carry off international prizes. A full listing of Irish farmhouse cheeses would occupy more space than is available, but we can note the better-known brands.

Ardrahan. A semi-soft cheese made in Co. Cork from pasteurized cow's milk on a farm with a herd of 200 Friesian cattle. It has won the title of Supreme Champion at the British Cheese Awards.

Ardsallagh. Goat's cheese from Co. Cork, made in both soft and hard varieties.

Cashel Blue. Made from pasteurized cow's milk with a vegetarian rennet, this has become one of the very best-known and widely loved Irish brands. There are many fine blues now made in Ireland but this was the first. As the name suggests, it is from Co. Tipperary.

Cooleeney. A soft cow's cheese, similar in style to Camembert, from Co. Tipperary.

Durrus. A semi-soft cow's milk cheese from West Cork.

Gubeen. One of the best-known Irish farmhouse cheeses, it's semi-soft, washed-rind and made from pasteurized cow's milk.

Killeen. From east Co. Galway; the proprietor is a Dutch woman who trained as a cheesemaker in the Netherlands before coming to Ireland. She produces both a goat's milk and a cow's milk cheese, similar in style to Dutch Gouda.

Milleens. From the Beara Peninsula in West Cork, this popular pasteurized cow's milk cheese with animal rennet is semi-soft with an attractive orange rind.

Meat

The traditional staples of beef, lamb, mutton, pork and bacon are still the backbone of the Irish diet. More inventive recipes have been developed in recent decades, as the food revolution has progressed. That said, it is still depressing to encounter carveries in pubs and hotels all serving the same roasts of meat, two veg and potatoes in various disguises and garnished with brown gravy. This traditional, unimaginative but perhaps reassuring meal remains popular; old habits die hard.

Vegetarians

There is a growing number of vegetarians in Ireland, as evidenced by the increase in the number of vegetarian restaurants and health-food shops, especially in the larger urban centres. That said, many vegetarians feel that the choice they are offered in ordinary restaurants is very limited. But it is a growing market and restaurant menus will have to reflect that growth.

The general consensus is that Café Paradiso in Cork is the best vegetarian restaurant in Ireland. A comprehensive listing of all the vegetarian and vegan restaurants in Ireland can be found at www. happycow.net.

10

Places to See and Things to Do

Apart from the three UNESCO World Heritage Sites at Newgrange, Skellig Michael and the Giant's Causeway (see p. 6), there are many other experiences that the visitor should not miss. Here is a short list of the essential ones. Of its nature, this is not exhaustive. Rather, it constitutes a sort of 'best of'. We'll begin with the principal cities and towns and then take a selective tour of the rest of the country.

***

Dublin

***

THE GUINNESS STOREHOUSE

In the heart of the St James's Gate brewery complex, this is the single biggest visitor attraction in the Irish capital. Housed in the seven-storey former fermentation plant, it tells you everything you could possibly want to know about Ireland's national beverage. You can finish off in the Gravity Bar at the top of the house where you get a complimentary pint of the black stuff.

TRINITY COLLEGE AND THE BOOK OF KELLS

Located plumb in the city centre. The west front entrance, facing College Green and Dame Street, dates from 1759 and most of the buildings in Front Square, just inside the entrance, are of the same period. Trinity's most famous treasure is the Book of Kells, which is kept in the Old Library building. An illuminated manuscript containing a Latin translation of the Four Gospels, it was found in the Co. Meath town of Kells, a noted Columban site, but was probably composed on the island of Iona in the Inner Hebrides where St Columba – Columkille in the Irish spelling – had his principal monastery. The Book of Kells has been in the safe keeping of Trinity since the seventeenth century.

Trinity College is the work of many hands. Its west front, designed by Theodore Jacobson (1759) leads to Front Square. Here the chapel and examination hall, facing each other, are by Sir William Chambers, who never set a foot in Ireland: he sent the plans over from London. Richard Castle designed the little Printing House and the Dining Hall. The Old Library is dated to 1712 and is the work of Sir Thomas Burgh. The roof was originally flat but the sensational barrel vault was added by Deane and Woodward in the 1860s, a piece of Victorian swagger that would not be permitted today under planning laws. The same architectural practice was responsible for the Museum Building (1852), with echoes of Venetian Gothic that also crop up in their Kildare Street Club (now the Alliance Française) just across the street from the College Park. The Campanile, designed by Sir Charles Lanyon, dates from 1853. The Graduates Memorial Building (1897) is the work of Sir Thomas Drew. The oldest building in Trinity is the terrace called The Rubrics (c.1700) that separates Front Square from New Square. The new library (1970) and the Arts Building are successful modern additions.

THE GALLERIES AND MUSEUMS

The National Gallery of Ireland on Merrion Square has just completed a splendid renovation. A separate entrance around the corner on Clare Street gives direct access to the distinguished extension completed some years ago. Further up along Merrion Square is the Natural History Museum, known popularly as the Dead Zoo, a fascinating and quaint exhibition. The National Museum of Ireland has two sites in the city: the archaeological collection, including artefacts from pre-Christian times, is in Kildare Street; the military and decorative arts collection is located in the former Collins Barracks complex in Benburb Street, towards the west of the city centre. The Dublin City Gallery on Parnell Square, better known as the Hugh Lane in memory of its principal benefactor, has a distinguished collection of Impressionist masterpieces. The Chester Beatty Library, with its outstanding collection of Oriental and Islamic art and artefacts, is in the grounds of Dublin Castle. The Little Museum of Dublin on St Stephen's Green is a gem, the essential city record.

DUBLIN CASTLE is something of a misnomer. It isn't a castle in the ordinary sense of the word but a series of administrative and ceremonial buildings that have grown organically over centuries. It was the epicentre of English power in Ireland and its handover to the forces of the new Irish Free State in 1922 was a deeply symbolic moment.

THE CATHEDRALS. Near the Castle are the two principal cathedrals, Christ Church and St Patrick's. Christ Church was the very centre of the original Viking city; it dates from 1038. St Patrick's, although nearby, was outside the city walls. It dates from 1190. Both cathedrals were heavily restored in the nineteenth century, with Sir Thomas Drew as consulting architect in each case. Little of the medieval fabric survives in either cathedral, although the crypt in Christ Church is an exception to that rule. Drew was also responsible for St Anne's Cathedral, Belfast and a number of minor public buildings in Dublin.

THE CASINO – means 'little house' in Italian and is definitely not a gambling house – at Marino is off the beaten track, surrounded by unsympathetic and drab housing off the Malahide Road in the northern suburbs. None the less, it is well worth a detour. Built as a country retreat in the eighteenth century for the extremely wealthy Lord Charlemont, it is by far the finest neoclassical building in Ireland, full of architectural quirks and surprises.

THE DART is the commuter rail line that generally hugs the coast. One of the odd things about Dublin city centre is that it gives you little idea of how close to the sea you are. The DART (Dublin Area Rapid Transit) solves that problem. Running south, all trains go to Bray but every alternate one continues to the next station down the line, Greystones, which is your best option. The bay opens up on your left shortly after Sydney Parade station; the view of Killiney Bay south of Dalkey station is stunning; and the last leg, between Bray and Greystones, offers fine marine views. Going north, the line divides at Howth Junction, with every other train going to Malahide or Howth. Choose Howth, a fishing village with lots of good restaurants and excellent walking options at the northern end of Dublin Bay.

Belfast

TITANIC BELFAST. The Belfast shipyard of Harland & Wolff built the most famous and ill-fated of all ships. On the site of the old shipyard, this recent museum, housed in a stunning building, has quickly become the city's principal visitor attraction.

ST ANNE'S CATHEDRAL, designed by the ubiquitous Sir Thomas Drew, is the finest piece of ecclesiastical architecture in the city. Its steel Spire of Hope was added in 2007.

THE CITY HALL is the most prominent building in Belfast city centre. Standing on the site of the old White Linen Hall, it is the finest example of assertive Victorian civic architecture in Ireland. It echoes the great town halls of the north of England in the heyday of the industrial revolution: Manchester, Leeds, Bradford. Nineteenth-century Belfast and environs were the only part of Ireland where heavy industry established itself. The City Hall is a monument to the city's glory years and a reminder that nineteenth-century east Ulster was really a westerly extension of the industrial heartlands of northern England and the west of Scotland.

THE ULSTER MUSEUM, together with the nearby Queen's University and the Botanic Gardens, with its Victorian palm house and tropical ravine, make this part of south Belfast well worth a visit. The area is easily reached from the city centre by bus or taxi.

CRUMLIN ROAD JAIL was notorious, not least because of its frequent mentions during the troubles. But it closed in 1996 and in 2013 it was transformed into a museum and visitor attraction, part of the clever use Belfast has made of the peace dividend.

STORMONT in the eastern suburbs of Belfast is the site of the devolved Northern Ireland Assembly. Built in 1932 to house the old parliament of Northern Ireland, it is very splendid – far too splendid for its purpose: seldom has such an exiguous assembly possessed such lavish quarters. Even as it stands, it is a pared-down version of an even more megalomaniacal plan which had to be abandoned in economic hard times.

Cork

THE ENGLISH MARKET in the city centre is by a mile the finest food market in Ireland. The present enclosure dates from 1862 but required significant restoration and redevelopment following serious fires in 1980 and 1986. It has won a Europa Nostra award for architectural preservation. It emphasizes yet again Cork's pivotal position in the history of the Irish provision trade.

ST FIN BARRE'S CATHEDRAL is named for the city's patron saint. The diocesan cathedral of the Anglican diocese of Cork, Cloyne and Ross, this distinctive building dates from 1870 and maintains a dramatic presence on the south branch of the River Lee. On the opposite north side of the river, the church of St Anne's, Shandon has a set of bells that inspired the poem 'The Bells of Shandon', 'that sound so grand on / the pleasant waters of the River Lee'.

THE CRAWFORD in Emmet Place is the city's leading art gallery. It houses an interesting and well-exhibited collection.

FOTA WILDLIFE PARK is found to the east of the city and is worth a day trip. Not far away is the pretty small town of Cobh (pron. Cove), the original Cove of Cork, from which transatlantic liners carried generations of Irish people into American exile. It was also the last port visited by the ill-fated Titanic.

GOUGANE BARRA is a settlement well to the west of the city, near the county border with Kerry. The River Lee rises here but its real point of interest is St Finbarr's Oratory, as it is believed to be, which occupies a small island in the lake. There is a forest park and a waymarked walking trail here as well.

Limerick

KING JOHN'S CASTLE is one of the most formidable Norman structures in Ireland. Built to protect the upper reaches of the Shannon estuary as it begins to open out towards the Atlantic, it was built in the thirteenth century. It has been renovated and reopened as a major tourist attraction in recent years.

BUNRATTY CASTLE is near Limerick city, on the road to Ennis in Co. Clare. It is a large tower house originally dating from 1425, one of the biggest of its kind in the country. Tower houses were built for defence and signify an unsettled countryside, as distinct from manor houses or other unfortified structures. The sheer bulk of Bunratty, however, justifies the use of the word castle. It was a stronghold of the O'Briens, earls of Thomond. In subsequent centuries many decorative features were added and it was fully restored in the 1950s. An adjacent folk park has been created.

THE HUNT MUSEUM is named for John and Gertrude Hunt, dealers in antiquities who built up an exceptional private collection focused on medieval decorative arts. The Hunt family donated the collection to the Irish state; the museum is in the old Limerick Custom House.

LOUGH GUR is to the south of the town, near the village of Bruff. The site of a heritage park, it traces the different ages of human settlement here from the Neolithic age onwards.

Galway

EYRE SQUARE and HIGH STREET / QUAY STREET represent the centre of this compact city. Just off Shop Street stands the Collegiate Church of St Nicholas, which is worth a visit. The same cannot be said for the Catholic Galway Cathedral which dates from 1965: it's big, derivative and vulgar.

CONNEMARA NATIONAL PARK is in the wild and beautiful country-side to the west of the city. A huge, rugged landscape dominated by the mountains known as the Twelve Bens, it is one of the leading visitor attractions in Ireland. The southern end of Connemara, along the shore of Galway Bay, is a Gaeltacht area.

THE BURREN is an area of north Co. Clare, on the southern shore of Galway Bay and easily accessible by car from Galway itself. It is a landscape unique in north-west Europe, an exposed area of limestone karst which gives the appearance of a moonscape. In the small crevices between the limestone pavements, rare plants otherwise seen only in Mediterranean and Alpine settings flourish. The area occupies more than 200 sq km.

THE ARAN ISLANDS are in Galway Bay and are officially assigned to Co. Galway but geologically they are an extension of the Burren. There are three islands, Inishmore, Inishmaan and Inisheer. There are ancient remains on the islands, none more impressive than the great Bronze Age enclosure of Dún Aonghasa on Inishmore. There are ferry services from the village of Rossaveal, west of Galway city, to Kilronan, the principal settlement on Inishmore.

Around the Country

THE ROCK OF CASHEL, just outside the Co. Tipperary town of the same name, was the traditional seat of the Gaelic kings of Munster and later became an important ecclesiastical site. Its collection of buildings stand on a rocky promontory that commands the surrounding plain. The most visible structure is the round tower; the most significant is Cormac's Chapel, one of the few examples of pure Romanesque architecture in Ireland.

HOLYCROSS ABBEY, not far from Cashel in the same county, is the best-preserved and best-restored Cistercian abbey in Ireland. It was founded in the late twelfth century by Dónal Mór O'Brien, the King of Munster.

THE CLIFFS OF MOHER on the coast of Co. Clare are among the top visitor attractions in the country. There is car parking and a visitor centre but the stunning views are best enjoyed al fresco. At their highest point, they rise over 700 feet above the sea.

THE RING OF KERRY is a drive that takes you around the Iveragh Peninsula, the middle of the three peninsulas in the county. Driving anticlockwise, you start at the town of Killorglin, proceeding west along the southern shore of Dingle Bay before turning south at the town of Cahersiveen and reaching Caherdaniel on the northern shore of the Kenmare River, actually an estuarial inlet of the Atlantic Ocean. Nearby is Derrynane, country seat of Daniel O'Connell. From here, the route doubles back to the east to reach the pretty town of Kenmare before taking the beautiful road through the Macgillycuddy's Reeks to reach Killarney, fabled since the nineteenth century as Heaven's Reflex and reckoned by many to be among the most beautiful landscapes in the world.

GLENDALOUGH is an early Christian monastic site set in a beautiful valley in the heart of Co. Wicklow. The name is an anglicization of a Gaelic place name meaning the valley of the two lakes, which indeed there are. The site is still in a good state of preservation, with many further ecclesiastical buildings added up to the Reformation. In its early days it was associated with the piously ascetic St Kevin, who is supposed to have thrown a beautiful young temptress into the lake rather than compromise his celibacy. The moment is recalled in a ballad: 'He gave the poor craythur a shake / And I wish a policeman had caught him. / He threw her right into the lake / and – bejaysus she sank to the bottom.' Glendalough is accessible by car from the south Dublin suburb of Rathfarnham by taking the road over the Featherbed Mountain, along the old Military Road past the Sally Gap before descending through Glenmacnass into Glendalough. You'll find it hard to think that you are less than an hour by car from a capital city.

DRUMCLIFF is a village just north of Sligo and is the site of an ancient monastery. Its fame rests on the fact that W.B. Yeats is buried in the churchyard there: 'Under bare Ben Bulben's head / In Drumcliff churchyard Yeats is laid'. It is also an excellent vantage point for looking at bare Ben Bulben's head. This great wedge-shaped mountain is the western end of a series of mountains and hills that span a couple of counties immediately to the east. Visually, it can claim to be the most dramatic mountain in the country.

ARMAGH is the ecclesiastical capital of Ireland, the seat of both the Roman Catholic and Anglican primates. Its two cathedrals are each dedicated to St Patrick, whose historic association with the place gave it its status and prestige, cognate with that of Canterbury in England. However, Armagh is worth seeing because of its remodelling in the eighteenth century: it is one of the prettier classical townscapes in Ireland. The central Mall is particularly pleasing. In Armagh Planetarium you can take a walk through the solar system in its Astropark or tour the night sky in the Digital Theatre.

SHANNON CRUISES. The Shannon is fully navigable for most of its course. The main river can be cruised from Carrick-on-Shannon in Co. Leitrim down to Killaloe, Co. Clare, just outside Limerick city. Even better, the reopening of the Ballyconnell canal, which had fallen into disuse, in 1993 opened up a route east of Carrick that gave access to the Upper and Lower Lough Erne system in Northern Ireland; it has been one of the most benign examples of cross-border co-operation. This inland waterway system is one of the very finest ways to see Ireland.

11
NOT LITERATURE

This chapter deals with all the plastic arts, using the term generously. In short, everything that is not literature, the one thing for which Ireland is especially well known.

Architecture

JAMES GANDON (1742–1823) was born in London and came to Ireland in 1781. No architect has had a more profound effect on the Irish landscape, particularly that of the capital. His two great buildings are the **Custom House** and the **Four Courts**, both on the north quays of the Liffey.

The Custom House was started in 1781 and opened for business ten years later. It moved a critical part of the city's infrastructure downriver towards the bay: the previous custom house had been situated upriver nearer to the medieval core of the city near Christ Church Cathedral. The new building generated considerable controversy because it was sponsored by the powerful Beresford family who owned the site. The result, however, is the finest classical building in Dublin. It was burnt by the IRA during the War of Independence and subsequently restored. However, the slender dome, originally of Portland stone, was restored using the cheaper Ardbracken stone.

The Four Courts, further upriver on the north quays, was completed in 1796. It is more monumental than the Custom House, dominated by the huge central drum that provides a roof for the central rotunda beneath, known as the round hall. It too was destroyed, this time in the civil war in 1922, and subsequently restored.

Other notable Gandon buildings in Dublin are the **King's Inns**, the training school for barristers, and the eastern extension of the Parliament House (now the Bank of Ireland, College Green) which projects over the pavement in Westmoreland Street.

EDWARD LOVETT PEARCE (1699–1733), whose father was a first cousin of Sir John Vanbrugh who designed Blenheim Palace in Oxfordshire, was responsible for the Parliament House on College Green, later augmented by Gandon. The earliest monumental public building in modern Dublin, it was begun in 1729.

FRANCIS JOHNSTON (1760–1839), born in Armagh, designed the General Post Office (GPO) in O'Connell Street (1818) and a number of distinguished country houses.

THOMAS COOLEY (1740–84) was the English architect who designed the Royal Exchange, now the City Hall.

The **Georgian Squares** and their surrounding streets are the most characteristic features of classical Dublin. The earliest, **Merrion Square**, dates from 1752. It was designed by John Ensor for the Fitzwilliam Estate, which developed this whole southside Georgian area, culminating in **Fitzwilliam Square** and environs which was not completed until the 1820s. Two of the finest streetscapes in Ireland are in this area: the long panorama of Fitzwilliam Street Upper and Fitzwilliam Place; and the view along Merrion Square South and Upper Mount Street (c.1820) which is enclosed by St Stephen's Church (1824) known universally as the Pepper Canister. On the north side, **Mountjoy Square** (1792–1818) has suffered from the sad neglect that has blighted the north inner city in modern times.

Outside Dublin, the finest and most coherent expression of Georgian planning is in **Newtown Pery** in **Limerick**. In the 1760s, this was open country running down to the River Shannon. The owner, Edmund Sexton Pery, asked an architect called Davis Ducart – actually Daviso du Arcort: he was Sardinian – to plan a new town there. Newtown Pery is now the centre of the city of Limerick.

In **Cork**, the **quadrangle in University College** dates from the earliest days of the university (founded 1845) and was designed by the practice of Deane and Woodward, the pre-eminent architects of mid-Victorian Ireland.

In **Galway**, the quadrangle at NUIG (National University of Ireland Galway, formerly University College Galway) is based on Christ Church Oxford and dates from 1849.

In **Belfast**, the City Hall is the showpiece building in the city centre and an exuberant example of British municipal architecture. Queen's University (1845) is a pleasing campus in confident mid-Victorian style. Sir Charles Lanyon (1813–89) was the principal architect of Victorian Belfast. Among his many achievements, the main building at Queen's (1849) is best known, although he also designed the Palm House in the Botanic Gardens. Crumlin Road Gaol and courthouse are further examples of his work. As County Surveyor of Co. Antrim (1836–42) he made an important input into the construction of the Antrim Coast Road. Nor was his work confined to Ulster: he designed the Campanile in Front Square in Trinity College Dublin (1853). The Titanic Centre is the latest addition to the city's infrastructure. The Waterfront Hall (1989–97) is a concert venue built in the depths of the troubles, designed by local architects, and was a vote of confidence in the future at a distressed moment in the city's history.

In **Derry**, the most remarkable human artefact is not a building but the city walls which girdle the centre. The walls are intact. It was the last walled city or town built anywhere in Europe (1613–18). The defence of the city by supporters of King William III against the besieging troops of King James II in 1689 gave the city its foundation myth. The repelling of the siege left the small Protestant town – as it then was – unviolated: the Maiden City. By the early twentieth century, Derry had long lost its Protestant majority but a shameless and ingenious system of gerrymandering maintained unionist control of the local council until the outbreak of the troubles in the late 1960s.

At **Clonmacnoise**, on the eastern bank of the River Shannon just south of Athlone, lie the ruins of the most extensive early Christian monastic site in Ireland. This is the point at which the principal east–west route in ancient Ireland crossed the river, which in turn marked the boundary between the provinces of Leinster and Connacht. Being so close to that boundary, it drew patronage from both provinces. Its foundation date is usually given as the 540s. It lasted for a millennium, until the fury of the Reformation did for it. English troops sailed down from Athlone in 1552 and laid it waste. Still, even in its current state, it is mighty impressive. Its centrepieces are two round towers and three high crosses.

Public Sculpture

The principal street in Dublin is O'Connell Street, just north of the River Liffey. At either end are statues of the two great nineteenth-century giants of Irish nationalism, Daniel O'Connell and Charles Stewart Parnell.

The O'Connell Monument is at the southern end of the street, by the river. It was the work of John Henry Foley (1818–74), the leading Irish sculptor of his day. It was unveiled in 1882. The four winged figures on the monument represent Patriotism, Fidelity, Courage and Eloquence: they are the work of Thomas Brock. Foley was also responsible for the central figure of Prince Albert in the Albert Memorial in London.

At the northern end of the street, the Parnell Monument was designed by Augustus Saint-Gaudens (1848–1907) who, although born in Dublin, was reared in the United States and did most of his distinguished work there.

The Spire, standing at the point in O'Connell Street once occupied by the Nelson Pillar, is the work of Ian Ritchie. It is completely abstract, without any overt symbolic or political message.

Other statues on O'Connell Street, moving from south to north:

William Smith O'Brien (1803–64), patriot
Sir John Gray (1816–75), newspaper publisher and promoter
    of the first piped water scheme for Dublin
James Larkin (1876–1947), labour leader
Fr Theobald Mathew (1790–1856), temperance campaigner

Other prominent Dublin statues:

Henry Grattan (1746–1820), patriot, College Green
Thomas Davis (1814–45), patriot, College Green

Robert Emmet (1778–1803), patriot, St Stephen's Green
West
Theobald Wolfe Tone (1763–98), patriot, corner of
St Stephen's Green North and East
James Joyce (1882–1941), writer, top of North Earl Street
Oscar Wilde (1854–1900), writer, corner of Merrion Square
West and North
Patrick Kavanagh (1904–67), poet, Grand Canal bank near
Baggot Street Bridge
James Connolly (1868–1916), patriot, Beresford Place
Famine Memorial, Custom House Quay
Children of Lir, Garden of Remembrance, Parnell Square
Phil Lynott (1949–86), musician, Harry Street

Prominent public sculptures and statues outside Dublin:

Father Theobald Mathew (1790–1856), temperance
campaigner, Patrick Street, Cork
National Monument, Grand Parade, Cork
Galway Hookers Monument, Eyre Square, Galway
Commodore John Barry, Crescent Quay, Wexford

Fine Art

Although not renowned as a centre of fine art, Ireland has none the
less produced some accomplished painters. The following list, in
roughly chronological order, acknowledges the better-known ones.

Charles Jervas (1675–1739) was a pupil of Godfrey Kneller in
London and succeeded him as principal painter to King George I.
He also painted one of the best-known portraits of Jonathan Swift.

The Swiss-Italian stuccoists **Paul** (1695–1176) and **Philip** (1702–79)
Lafranchini were responsible for some of the very finest Irish
plasterwork of the eighteenth century. Their work can still be seen
in a number of great Irish houses.

James Barry (1741–1806) was born in Cork; he was a friend of Edmund Burke and a professor in the Royal Academy until he was expelled for views regarded as too friendly to the French Revolution. He was one of the leading neoclassical painters in late eighteenth-century Britain.

James Malton (c.1764–1803) was born in London but moved to Dublin as a young man. His twenty-five views of the city are the best visual record we have of Dublin in its golden age.

William Ashford (1746–1824) was the first President of the Royal Hibernian Academy.

Nathaniel Hone the elder (1718–84) was one of the founders of the Royal Academy in London and the first of a distinguished line of painters and artists.

James Arthur O'Connor (1792–1841) was the leading Irish landscape painter of his day. His masterpiece *A Thunderstorm: the Frightened Wagoner* is in the National Gallery of Ireland.

Daniel Maclise (1806–70) was a Romantic history painter and a friend of Charles Dickens, whose portrait he painted. Two of his large murals, commemorating the meeting of Wellington and Blücher at Waterloo and the death of Nelson, hang in the Houses of Parliament in London. His best-known Irish work, *The Marriage of Strongbow and Aoife* (1854) is in the National Gallery of Ireland.

Walter Osborne (1859–1903) was a painter of portraits and urban landscapes. As a young artist, he spent time in Flanders and Brittany, learning the techniques of open air painting which carried his later work towards a form of impressionism.

Sir John Lavery (1856–1941) was among the most successful society portrait painters of his day. One of his many portraits of his wife Hazel adorned Irish banknotes for more than forty years.

Roderic O'Conor (1860–1940) spent most of his career in France and was influenced by the Impressionists and post-impressionists, especially Van Gogh and Gauguin.

William Orpen (1878–1931) was born in Dublin but made his career in England, with notable success. He was an official war artist during World War I and painted two large canvases showing the negotiations and signing of the Treaty of Versailles.

Louis le Brocquy (1916–2012) was the most significant Irish artist of the second half of the twentieth century. He was particularly renowned for his sensitive head portraits of leading literary figures.

Colin Middleton (1910–83) and **Basil Blackshaw** (1932–2016) are two of the most accomplished modern Ulster artists, while their southern contemporary **Tony O'Malley** (1913–2003) was a brilliant abstract colourist.

Film

Until the 1980s, the Irish film industry barely existed. But the emergence of a talented generation of film-makers transformed the scene. The first two to win widespread critical acclaim and commercial success were Neil Jordan and Jim Sheridan. Other directors, such as Paddy Breathnach, followed. Breathnach's *I Went Down* (1997) was a breakthrough movie for the actor Brendan Gleeson, who went on to be an international star.

Other Irish actors followed. Colin Farrell, Liam Neeson, Cillian Murphy, Saoirse Ronan and others have all gone on to stardom.

However, the two Irish film directors with the longest international reach and the greatest body of achievement over a period of twenty years and more are Jordan and Sheridan. Neil Jordan is a novelist and short-story writer as well as a film-maker. He has written as well as directed some of his best films, among them *Angel* (1982), *The Company of Wolves* (1984), *The Crying Game* (1992) and *Michael Collins* (1996). He won an Oscar for Best Original Screenplay for *The Crying Game* and was also nominated for Best Director.

Jim Sheridan's breakthrough movie was *My Left Foot* (1989), based on the life of the severely disabled Dublin writer Christy

Brown. The part of Christy Brown was played by Daniel Day-Lewis in a bravura performance that won him the Oscar for Best Actor while Brenda Fricker, playing Brown's mother, took the Oscar for Best Supporting Actress. Sheridan himself was nominated for Best Director and, as co-writer, for Best Adapted Screenplay. Other nominations and awards followed for In the Name of the Father (1993), The Boxer (1997) and In America (2003).

Music

The most auspicious date in Irish musical history is 13 April 1742. On that date, at the New Musick Hall in Fishamble Street in Dublin, the first ever performance of Handel's Messiah was given. The composer himself was the conductor.

Ireland has produced a number of minor classical composers, the most significant of whom was John Field (1782–1837). He spent most of his musical career, both as pianist and composer, in Russia. He is generally credited with having developed the nocturne, later brought to perfection by Chopin.

The country is, however, celebrated for its rich tradition of folk music. An important event in the capturing and transmission of that tradition occurred in 1792. This was the three-day Belfast Harp Festival. Ten Irish and one Welsh harpist competed for prizes. The real significance of the event was the presence of the music collector Edward Bunting (1773–1843), whose careful musical annotations of the airs played at the festival ensured the survival of the Irish harp tradition, at a time when it was feared it might die.

The cultural revival of the 1890s had an important musical element. The first Feis Ceoil (music festival) took place in 1897, focusing on both formal and traditional music. The influence of the Gaelic League and other revivalist organizations also helped to sustain the Irish folk tradition.

A further advance occurred in the 1960s with the formation of the traditional group Ceoltóirí Chualann by the composer Seán

Ó Riada, out of which emerged The Chieftains, who brought a degree of musical sophistication to the traditional repertoire that has won them international acclaim.

In rock music, the late Rory Gallagher (1948–95) formed Taste in 1969 and became one of the leading guitarists in the world. Van Morrison (1945–) is simply one of the greatest singer-songwriters of the age. U2, formed in Dublin in 1976, can lay claim to being the leading rock band in the world.

12
SPORT

Gaelic Games

These are Gaelic football, hurling, camogie (ladies' hurling) and handball. The games are administered by the Gaelic Athletic Association (GAA), which claims to be the largest amateur sporting body in the world. The declared motivation for the founding of the GAA in 1884 was to restore and preserve the ancient game of hurling. In that, it has been successful, although the greater popularity of football was established from an early date.

The GAA promotes the Irish language and Irish culture. In its early years it was dominated by Fenians, the most radical of nationalist elements, and it has never completely lost that inclination, although it is much diluted in more recent times. Its nationalism assumed a culture of exclusion and introversion when, in 1902, it passed rule 27 which read: 'any member of the Association who plays or encourages in any way rugby, football, hockey or any imported game which is calculated to injuriously affect our national pastimes is suspended from the Association'. Cricket was soon added to the list of proscribed sports. Rule 27 survived until 1971. Its repeal symbolized the more open Ireland of the 1960s in contrast to the introverted decades following independence.

The Ban, as it was known, had its absurdities. Douglas Hyde, the first President of Ireland and a founder of the Gaelic League, had his GAA membership rescinded for attending an international soccer match as part of his presidential duties. One very distinguished hurler – an All-Ireland medal winner – was banned for attending a fund-raising dance at a local soccer club.

If the GAA could seem paranoid, it sometimes had cause. Its most traumatic day was Bloody Sunday, 21 November 1920. That morning, in the middle of the War of Independence, Michael Collins' hit men, the Squad, raided the homes of suspected British intelligence agents. They killed fourteen of them and wounded six more. In retaliation, a party of Auxiliaries, a hastily assembled paramilitary police reserve, opened fire on players and spectators at a football match at Croke Park, the GAA headquarters in Dublin. Thirteen died, including one player, and sixty were injured. One of the principal stands in Croke Park is named for the dead player, Michael Hogan of Tipperary.

That day lived long in the GAA's memory. When Lansdowne Road, the principal rugby stadium, was being rebuilt in the early 2000s, a motion to open Croke Park up to 'other sports' was carried but only after long and impassioned opposition. When England played rugby there for the first time in 2007, the singing of 'God Save the Queen' was a particularly fraught moment. Happily, the crowd were impeccably well behaved. There was a moment of low comedy outside the stadium when some brat brandishing a protest placard saying 'No Foreign Games' was himself wearing a Glasgow Celtic replica shirt.

Gaelic football is the most popular spectator sport in Ireland. In terms of actual participation, soccer is now probably close to it, although reliable statistics for playing numbers are not available. However, when it comes to filling stadiums, nobody can touch the GAA. The All-Ireland final, played every September, is guaranteed to fill Croke Park, whose capacity of 82,300 makes it the third-largest stadium in Europe behind the Camp Nou in Barcelona and Wembley in London.

The game was codified in the early days of the GAA. It evolved from a whole series of regional and local kickabouts, just as most modern sports have done. Prior to the development of the railways, there was little point in having sports codified to a national standard. The basic unit of the GAA is the local club, usually associated with the local Roman Catholic parish. There is hardly a parish in Ireland without a club, and football – unlike hurling – flourishes in every corner.

The clubs are organized first at county level and then provincially. Each county championship winning club proceeds to represent the county in the provincial championship. The four provincial champions then play semi-finals and final to determine the all-Ireland winning club. The club final is played in Croke Park on 17 March, St Patrick's Day.

From the clubs, the best players go on to play at inter-county level. The county game, which is the one that really draws the crowds, is first organized provincially and then nationally. The championship was first played in 1887 and has been contested every year since. The season runs from May to September, with the provincial championships generally settled by late July. The All-Ireland semi-finals are played off by the provincial champions in August, with the final usually on the third Sunday in September.

Until recent years, the championship was played on a pure knockout basis. This further damaged already weak counties – small counties with correspondingly small playing populations – who might play one championship match all year. To alleviate this, a 'back-door' system has been introduced, whereby counties beaten in the early rounds can get a second chance. One of the problems for weaker counties is that there is no transfer system in the GAA: you play for the county where you grew up. It means, of course, that some of the game's very finest players down the years have never had a sniff of championship honours. It's tough being an isolated talent.

Kerry is the most successful Gaelic football county. It has won the championship 37 times at the time of writing. The only other county even in double figures is Dublin, with 26 wins. However, unlike hurling, the football championship has gone right around the country. Teams from every province have won it. In all, 19 of the 32 counties have been victorious at least once since 1887.

The trophy is called the Sam Maguire Cup, to commemorate a man who was a prominent early member of the GAA, especially among Irish exiles in London. It is a replica of the Ardagh Chalice, one of the greatest of the Ireland's early Christian surviving arte-facts, rendered in silver.

The game itself is played by two teams of fifteen. Championship matches last for seventy minutes with one interval. Other matches are thirty minutes each way. The posts are H-shaped, like rugby, but the bottom part is netted. A point is scored if the ball, which is round like a soccer ball, is kicked or punched over the bar. A goal, which is worth three points, is scored when the ball is kicked or punched into the net. The scoring system is expressed in goals and points. Thus 2–10 (16 points) is not enough to beat 1–14 (17 points).

The sport which might be thought of as the nearest analogue to Gaelic Football is Australian Rules. Despite the differences between the two – Aussie Rules is professional and played with an oval ball – a hybrid game mixing the two sports has been developed and the so-called 'international rules' games between the two countries began in the 1990s. They continue from time to time despite occasional Irish complaints about the over-robust play of the Australians.

Hurling stands to Ireland rather as cricket does to England or baseball to the United States. It is widely acknowledged as the national game, the one that seems to express the national spirit more completely than any other. Yet, like the other two, it is not the most popular or widespread game in the country. Although played in every county, it is really a regional game. If you divide Ireland horizontally in two from Dublin to Galway, hurling is played seriously south of that line (although not with success in every county) and is much weaker north of the line.

The structure of the game is similar to football, as is the scoring system. There the similarities end. Hurling is a stick and ball game, incredibly fast at its best. Think of it as a speeded-up version of field hockey, but one where the hurley stick has an almost semicircular boss and the ball can be lifted and struck from the hand. It may not be carried by hand more than a few steps – a rule that is almost impossible to referee with consistency – but must be balanced on the boss of the stick while running at full tilt, for all the world like an egg-and-spoon race.

I have to restrain myself. I am a totally besotted fan because when it's good hurling is as good as any sport anywhere. It is reckoned to be the fastest field sport in the world; it is very skilful; it requires physical courage, although the danger of serious, disabling injury is very low. Championship hurling is played with a passion and commitment that can be almost frightening in its intensity. And the lads who play it are amateurs: they have jobs to go to the morning after. They'll be teaching your kids, or selling insurance or working down on the farm.

As to the championship, it has never been won by an Ulster county and only four times by a Connacht county. Even that county, Galway, now plays its championship hurling in Leinster because the standard in the rest of Connacht is so poor. Of the 129 championships contested since 1887, 93, or 72 per cent, have been won by three counties. Kilkenny lead the way with 36 titles, followed by Cork with 30 and Tipperary with 27. It is no accident that each county has a border with one of the others and Tipp has a border with both. The national game is really regional.

There is a further twist to this regionalism. The Scottish game of shinty evolved from an early version of hurling. Just as the early Irish brought the Gaelic language and Christianity to the west of Scotland and the Isles, so it brought this game. But it was an early Antrim version of hurling that migrated: modern shinty relates to hurling roughly as Scots Gaelic does to Irish. However, when hurling was codified by the early GAA, it was the south Leinster game that became normative. It may well be that the Antrim version, still retaining echoes of what became shinty, was bypassed. At all events, despite the game being played passionately in the Glens, Antrim have only ever reached the All-Ireland final twice and have lost both times. No other Ulster county plays at anything like top championship standard.

Soccer

Soccer is played in huge numbers but the domestic leagues draw very poor crowds. The game is administered in the Republic by the Football Association of Ireland (FAI) and in Northern Ireland by the Irish Football Association (IFA).

Both Irish international teams have had their moments. Northern Ireland reached the quarter-finals of the 1958 World Cup and also qualified for the 1982 and 1986 tournaments. They have not qualified since. As that NI team was fading, the ROI's glory years were beginning. The former England World Cup winner, Jack Charlton, was appointed manager of the team in 1986. Two years later, they qualified for their first ever European championship finals.

The tournament was held in Germany. The Republic were drawn against England in the first game. Against all expectations, they won 1–0. They then drew with Russia and lost to Holland and were eliminated, but victory over England was sufficient compensation.

They qualified for the next two World Cups, held respectively in Italy and the United States. In Italia 90, they played England once more. Gary Lineker opened the scoring for England but Kevin Sheedy equalized, and that is how it ended. They also drew with Egypt and Holland but it was enough to get them through to the second round against Romania.

No one who saw that game, which was just about the entire population of the Republic, will ever forget it. The game ended scoreless after extra time and it was settled on penalties. After four successful penalties each, the last Romanian penalty was taken by Daniel Timofte, a substitute. He hit it to Packie Bonner's right side but the big goalkeeper from Co. Donegal guessed right and made the save. The photograph of that moment is still regularly reproduced.

It meant that Ireland needed to convert their last penalty. It was taken by David O'Leary, also a substitute and a player whose relationship with Charlton was less than cordial. He hit it to the goalkeeper's left, the keeper went right and that was that: Ireland were in the quarter-finals of the World Cup.

They did not disgrace themselves. They lost 1–0 to the hosts, Italy, one of the giants of world football and the eventual winner of the tournament. The team's homecoming brought Dublin to a halt. It could hardly have been more lavish if Ireland had actually won the World Cup.

After that, 1994 was something of an anticlimax. None the less, the team had the satisfaction of beating Italy 1–0 in their opening game, thus gaining some degree of revenge for the defeat in Rome four years earlier. Ireland then lost to Mexico and drew with Norway. It was enough to get them through to the second round but there they succumbed to an excellent Dutch side.

Failure to qualify for Euro 96 marked the end of the Charlton era, by far the greatest in the history of Irish football. But more drama soon followed. He was succeeded by Mick McCarthy, the captain at Italia 90. The key player on the reconstituted team was the Manchester United midfielder, Roy Keane.

Keane, a Corkman, was uncompromising. He and McCarthy had a brittle relationship, not helped by the failure to qualify for either the 1998 World Cup or Euro 2000. However, ROI did qualify for the 2002 World Cup in Japan and South Korea. That is when the fireworks started.

The training facility for the Irish squad was on the island of Saipan in the Pacific, to the east of the Philippines. Keane thought that the training facilities were utterly inadequate and made his feelings known. He and McCarthy had a bitter exchange of words, which ended with Keane departing the squad and returning home before a ball was kicked in the tournament proper. The incident divided the nation.

After that, the results seemed almost secondary. In the event, the team reached the second round, only to be eliminated by Spain in a penalty shoot-out. But the aftershocks from the Saipan affair dominated the coverage. There were resignations in the FAI and McCarthy himself resigned towards the end of the year.

Since 2002, Ireland has qualified for only two major tournaments, Euro 2012 and 2016. They performed poorly at the first of these and while results were better in 2016, they failed to reach the quarter-finals.

Ireland's best players from both North and South play their football in the English and Scottish leagues. The English Premiership, in particular, has a large following in Ireland, with big support for Manchester United, Liverpool and Arsenal.

Rugby Union

Unlike soccer, this is organized on an all-Ireland basis. The Irish Rugby Football Union (IRFU), founded in 1880, merged two organizations that had existed since 1874, and has branches in each of the four provinces. Within each province, there is a club structure. The game is also played in schools, an important development nursery, and has traditionally been associated with fee-paying, middle-class schools.

Ireland's first international victory was against Scotland in 1881. It won the Triple Crown in 1894, beating England, Scotland and Wales in the same year. This was repeated in 1899 but not again until 1948 and 1949. By then, France had long since joined the annual European international championship so that the Triple Crown, while still regarded as an achievement, was eclipsed by the Grand Slam, in which the other four teams are all defeated in the same tournament. Ireland achieved this landmark in 1948 but has only repeated it only once, in 2009.

Triple Crowns	Grand Slams
1894	1948
1899	2009
1948	
1949	
1982	
1985	
2004	
2006	
2007	
2009	

Up to 1995, Rugby Union was an amateur game but in that year the game went professional. Ireland was initially reluctant to make this change but in fact the early days of the professional game were its most successful era, both internationally and at provincial level. While the international team continued to be selected on the basis of Irish birth or residential qualification, the provinces have reorganized as professional franchises.

The European club tournament, previously known as the Heineken Cup, was inaugurated in the 1995–96 season. Ulster became the first Irish province to win it, in 1999. Munster were beaten finalists in 2000 and 2002 and victory became a consuming ambition of the southern province. They finally reached their goal in 2006, repeating the feat in 2008. They were then eclipsed by Leinster, who won the tournament in 2009, 2011 and 2012.

Irish Heineken Cup Winners

1999	Ulster
2006	Munster
2008	Munster
2009	Leinster
2011	Leinster
2012	Leinster

Between Triple Crowns and a Grand Slam at international level and six victories in the premier European club tournament in thirteen years, the opening years of the twenty-first century have proved the most fertile in Irish rugby history. It was the era of the outside centre Brian O'Driscoll, Ireland's record try scorer at international level and beyond question the finest Irish back of the age. Paul O'Connell of Munster matched O'Driscoll's achievements in the forwards. Both men captained the British & Irish Lions touring sides.

Horse Racing

This is popular throughout the country and Ireland's reputation for breeding and training thoroughbreds is well established. There are twenty-five racecourses in ROI and two in NI.

Irish racing focuses on National Hunt races, over hurdles and fences, in the winter, while the summer months are devoted to the Flat. Although the Flat is more prestigious, the Irish passion for jump racing is undimmed. Nowhere is that better seen than at Cheltenham, where the annual National Hunt Festival, held every March and generally acknowledged as the supreme test of jumpers, draws an enormous Irish invasion.

The Grand National, run every year at Aintree near Liverpool, likewise attracts huge Irish interest. It is the most famous steeple-chase in the world.

The first Irish winner of the Cheltenham Gold Cup was Prince Regent in 1946, trained by Tom Dreaper. A further twenty-one Irish-trained horses have won the blue riband event to 2016. They include two hat-tricks: in 1948, 1949 and 1950 Vincent O'Brien trained Cottage Rake to successive Gold Cups. This feat was matched by Arkle, trained by Tom Dreaper, in 1964, 1965 and 1966. By general consent, Arkle is regarded as the greatest of all steeplechasers.

The two best-known racecourses for domestic National Hunt are Punchestown in Co. Kildare, whose annual festival is Ireland's answer to Cheltenham, and Fairyhouse in Co. Meath, where the Irish Grand National is run every Easter Monday.

On the Flat, the Irish Classics mirror their English equivalents, with The Curragh in Co. Kildare the principal course. The Irish Derby is run there, usually a few weeks after the Epsom Derby. For many years, Irish successes at Epsom were rare but since the 1960s they have become more frequent. This was particularly the case with the jockey–trainer partnership of Lester Piggott and Vincent O'Brien. Piggott was the greatest jockey of his era: four of his nine Derby winners – a record – were trained by O'Brien.

O'Brien was to training what Piggott was to riding. He met with consistent success both in National Hunt and on the Flat. He won the Cheltenham Gold Cup four times, including three years in a row (1948–50) with Cottage Rake. He also did the hat-trick in the Champion Hurdle (1949–51) with Hatton's Grace. In addition, he won the Grand National in 1953, 1954 and 1955 with three different horses.

When he switched to the Flat, O'Brien enjoyed equal success. He won the Epsom Derby six times over a twenty-year period as well as premium races in France and the United States. He retired in 1994 and died, aged 92, in 2009. His Ballydoyle yard was taken over by Aidan O'Brien – no relation – who is acknowledged as one of the world's leading trainers. He has won the Epsom Derby six times.

Among many other distinguished Irish training feats, one deserves special mention because it was widely thought to be impossible. Although Dermot Weld has also trained winners all over the racing world, his success in the Melbourne Cup in 1993 with Vintage Crop was the first ever win by a European trainer in Australia's most prestigious race. Not only that, but Weld repeated the achievement in 2002 with Media Puzzle.

Golf

This is a major participation sport in Ireland. The Golfing Union of Ireland has 430 affiliated clubs and the total playing number is estimated at 170,000. This is probably an underestimate because of proprietary clubs that are not affiliated to the GUI.

The growth of the sport in Ireland has coincided with a period of successes by Irish golfers in major international professional tournaments. Of the four Majors, the US Masters is still the only one not to have an Irish winner.

Irish Winners of Major Championships

2007	Pádraig Harrington	British Open
2008	Pádraig Harrington	British Open
2008	Pádraig Harrington	US PGA
2010	Graeme McDowell	US Open
2011	Rory McIlroy	US Open
2011	Darren Clarke	British Open
2012	Rory McIlroy	US PGA
2014	Rory McIlroy	British Open
2014	Rory McIlroy	US PGA

Olympic Games

Irish Olympic Gold Medallists

Pat O'Callaghan	Athletics	Hammer	Amsterdam	1928
Pat O'Callaghan	Athletics	Hammer	Los Angeles	1932
Bob Tisdall	Athletics	400m Hurdles	Los Angeles	1932
Ronnie Delany	Athletics	1500 Metres	Melbourne	1956
Michael Carruth	Boxing	Welterweight	Barcelona	1992
Michelle Smith	Swimming	400m Freestyle	Atlanta	1996
Michelle Smith	Swimming	200m Individual Medley	Atlanta	1996
Michelle Smith	Swimming	400m Individual Medley	Atlanta	1996
Katie Taylor	Boxing	Lightweight	London	2012

In addition, Ireland has won twelve silver and twelve bronze medals. Boxing has been Ireland's most successful Olympic sport.

Road Bowling

Irish road bowling involves a competition to propel a steel ball along a predetermined series of country roads, with the winner being the one who can complete the course in the fewest throws. The balls, sometimes called bullets, are three inches in diameter and weigh 28 ounces. They are therefore about the size of a cricket ball but much heavier.

The game is played mainly in counties Cork and Armagh. The ball is bowled underarm and skilled competitors can bowl with accuracy over hedges in order to take a bend in the road out of the equation. Competitions attract spectators and wagers are laid on possible winners.

13

INSTITUTIONS OF THE STATE(S)

Republic of Ireland

THE IRISH CONSTITUTION

The Anglo-Irish Treaty of 1921 created the Irish Free State, which later became the Republic. The constitution of the Free State was superseded by a new document, drafted under the direction of Éamon de Valera, in 1937. The new constitution was adopted by referendum on 1 July 1937. There were 685,105 votes in favour, 526,945 against. The constitution came into force on 29 December.

It declared Ireland to be 'a sovereign, independent, democratic state'. It also claimed jurisdiction over the territory of Northern Ireland but added that 'pending the re-integration of the national territory' laws would apply only in the 26 counties. The Irish language was given the status of first official language. The article guaranteeing freedom of religion none the less recognized 'the special position' of the Catholic Church in Irish life.

The legislature was named as the three houses of the Oireachtas, namely the President, the Dáil (lower house) and the Seanad (upper house). Of these, the Dáil is by far the most important, being the Irish equivalent of the House of Commons or the US House of Representatives. The government of the day is that which can command a majority in the Dáil. Amendments to the constitution can only be approved by referendum.

Over thirty amendments have been proposed since 1937. The most significant are these:

1959 & 1968	Unsuccessful proposals to amend the voting system from proportional representation to first past the post.
1972	Support for the accession treaty to join the EEC (later the EU).
1973	Reduction of the voting age from 21 to 18 and deletion of reference to the special position of the Catholic Church.

1983   Abortion: recognition of the right to life of the unborn.

1986   Provision to introduce divorce heavily defeated.

1996   Provision to introduce divorce carried narrowly.

In addition, referendums to ratify the EU treaties of Nice and Lisbon were first defeated but then carried on increased turnouts in later polls.

THE PRESIDENT

The President of Ireland is elected by national referendum for a seven-year term and acts as head of state. Apart from the normal ceremonial functions of a head of state, the President's principal function is to protect the constitution; this is done in consultation with the Council of State, an advisory body established under the constitution and comprising, among others, the Chief Justice, the President of the High Court and the Attorney-General. The President may refer a bill to the Supreme Court to test its constitutional status. No bill is law until signed by the President.

Presidents of Ireland

Douglas Hyde	1937–45
Sean T. O'Kelly	1945–59
Éamon de Valera	1959–73
Erskine Childers	1973–74
Cearbhaill Ó Dálaigh	1974–76
Patrick Hillery	1976–90
Mary Robinson	1990–97
Mary McAleese	1997–2011
Michael D. Higgins	2011–

THE TAOISEACH

The word means 'chieftain' in Irish and is the formal title of the prime minister under the 1937 Constitution. The deputy is called the Tánaiste. Between 1922 and 1937, under the terms of the 1922 Constitution, the head of government was referred to as the President of the Executive Council. This office was held by William

T. Cosgrave from 1922 to 1932 and then by Éamon de Valera until 1937. The following have held the office of Taoiseach:

1937–48	Éamon de Valera
1948–51	John A. Costello
1951–54	Éamon de Valera
1954–57	John A. Costello
1957–59	Éamon de Valera
1959–66	Seán Lemass
1966–73	Jack Lynch
1973–77	Liam Cosgrave
1977–79	Jack Lynch
1979–81	Charles J. Haughey
1981–82	Garret FitzGerald
1982	Charles J. Haughey
1982–87	Garret FitzGerald
1987–92	Charles J. Haughey
1992–94	Albert Reynolds
1994–97	John Bruton
1997–2008	Bertie Ahern
2008–11	Brian Cowen
2011–17	Enda Kenny
2017–	Leo Varadkar

THE GOVERNMENT

The government comprises a cabinet of fifteen persons with full ministerial status, assisted by ministers of state who are not in the cabinet. The Attorney-General and the government chief whip attend cabinet meetings, but without a vote. At the discretion of the Taoiseach, some ministers of state may also attend but not vote.

LOCAL GOVERNMENT

There are thirty-one local authorities in the Republic, three of which are city councils – Dublin, Cork and Galway – and the rest either county councils or joint city and county councils. Membership of each local authority is by election every five years. In addition, each authority has an executive head appointed by central government to act as CEO.

Local authorities are responsible for such functions as road maintenance, water supply and sewerage, planning and public libraries. Many responsibilities previously exercised by local authorities have been reserved to central government or to agencies appointed by them.

CIVIL SERVICE

Each government department is staffed by professional civil servants. The Irish Civil Service evolved from the British system, which had been radically reformed shortly before independence. The traditions and ethos of the British system find echoes in the Irish one. The head of each department is called the secretary-general and the secretary-general of the Department of the Taoiseach also acts as secretary to the government overall.

THE COURTS

In ascending order, these are:

District Courts
Circuit Court
Special Criminal Court
High Court
Court of Appeal
Supreme Court

Judges are appointed by the President on the advice of the government. Since the President has no personal discretion in the matter, the system is inherently political. However, the dangers of that system are mitigated by the establishment of the Judicial Appointments Advisory Board, which identifies potentially suitable candidates for judicial office and advises the government accordingly. It can send a number of names forward for final decision by the government.

Symbols

The official symbol of the Republic is the harp. A number of versions have been used in the Irish past, the best known being the eighteenth-century one that is now most commonly seen on the tail planes of Ryanair aircraft. The official emblem shows a stringed golden harp on a field of St Patrick's blue. Although green was adopted as the national colour in the nineteenth century, St Patrick's blue preceded it, being the colour chosen by the Order of St Patrick (1783), an Anglo-Irish equivalent for the English and Scottish chivalric orders of the Garter and the Thistle. The harp design is based on the so-called Trinity College harp, which is supposed to have been owned by Brian Ború.

The national flag is a tricolour of green, white and orange. It is meant to symbolize peace and reconciliation between the two historic traditions in Ireland.

Most Irish international sports teams adapt the shamrock as part of their logos.

Northern Ireland

Government

From 1920 to 1972, NI had a fully devolved system of one-party government with a regional prime minister, a cabinet and civil service. There were six prime ministers in that time:

Sir James Craig / Lord Craigavon	1921–40
John Miller Andrews	1940–43
Sir Basil Brooke / Lord Brookeborough	1943–63
Terence O'Neill	1963–69
James Chichester-Clark	1969–71
Brian Faulkner	1971–72

Under the pressures of the troubles, direct rule was instituted in 1972, with a secretary of state for Northern Ireland reporting to the cabinet in London. An effort to restore a form of power-sharing devolution – the Sunningdale Agreement of 1973 – succeeded in the short term but collapsed after a loyalist general strike paralysed the province.

SECRETARIES OF STATE FOR NORTHERN IRELAND

William Whitelaw	1972–73	Conservative
Francis Pym	1973–74	Conservative
Merlyn Rees	1974–76	Labour
Roy Mason	1976–79	Labour
Humphrey Atkins	1979–81	Conservative
James Prior	1981–84	Conservative
Douglas Hurd	1984–85	Conservative
Tom King	1985–89	Conservative
Peter Brooke	1989-92	Conservative
Sir Patrick Mayhew	1992–97	Conservative
Mo Mowlam	1997–99	Labour
Peter Mandelson	1999–2001	Labour
John Reid	2001–2	Labour
Paul Murphy	2002–5	Labour
Peter Hain	2005–7	Labour
Shaun Woodward	2007–10	Labour
Owen Paterson	2010–12	Conservative
Theresa Villiers	2012–16	Conservative
James Brokenshire	2016–	Conservative

The formal end of the troubles did not come until the Belfast Agreement of 1998. Even then, there were aftershocks. A power-sharing executive was suspended in 2002. A new agreement negotiated at St Andrews in Scotland in 2006 allowed a restored executive to be inaugurated in the following year. Remarkably, it meant that power in the province was now shared by the two parties on either side of the divide who had hitherto been most intransigent, the Democratic Unionists (DUP) and Sinn Féin.

The three first ministers have all been from the DUP: Ian Paisley, Peter Robinson and Arlene Foster. The deputy first minister to all three has been Martin McGuinness of Sinn Féin.

The Northern Ireland Assembly comprises 108 MLAs and meets at the old parliament building at Stormont in east Belfast.

LOCAL GOVERNMENT
There are eleven local government districts dealing with local administrative matters. This number represents a consolidation of the previously existing twenty-six district councils, an extraordinary number for a place not much bigger than Yorkshire. Their functions are limited; many administrative matters, such as housing, which are potentially sensitive are discharged by central agencies.

CIVIL SERVICE
There is an executive office and eight government departments. An independent body, the Civil Service Commissioners for Northern Ireland, ensures that public appointments are made on merit.

THE COURTS
In ascending order, these are:

Magistrates' Courts
County Courts
Crown Courts
High Court
Court of Appeal
Supreme Court of the UK

The system of appointing judges differs significantly from that in the Republic and is considerably more transparent. In the wake of the Belfast Agreement, a Northern Ireland Judicial Appointments Commission was established in 2005. It comprises eight members of the legal profession and five laypersons and makes one recommendation only to the Lord Chancellor in respect of each vacancy.

SYMBOLS
The official flag of Northern Ireland is the Union Flag of the UK, although the Irish tricolour is frequently displayed in nationalist areas and at Ulster GAA matches.

The so-called Ulster Banner shows a red cross on a white field, with the red hand symbol centred on the cross and a crown above it. It is associated exclusively with unionists and loyalists.

The red hand symbol is very ancient and has been associated with Ulster since prehistory. In early modern times, it became associated with the powerful O'Neills of Tyrone.

The emblem of the Police Service of Northern Ireland includes the Saltire of St Patrick, which is also included in the Union Flag to symbolize Ireland.

Flags and emblems remains a hugely sensitive and potentially contentious issue in the province.

14

RELIGION

The subject is unavoidable. It has coloured the Irish past and it still is the most visible outward sign of the communal divisions in Northern Ireland. So it be best to begin with a story which is probably apocryphal.

A Dublin wit, getting on in years, met a friend in the street who enquired after him. He replied: 'I am like an Irish census return, broken down by age, sex and religion.'

The Early Church

As we have seen (see p. 38), St Patrick, the national apostle, is the very first person in Ireland of whom we have some certain knowledge. Thus history – the reconstruction of the past from written sources, rather than from oral tall tales or myths – starts with the Christian moment.

The early Irish Church played an extraordinary role in the re-evangelization of Europe following the collapse of the Roman Empire in the west. From Iona in the Hebrides to Kiev in what is now the Ukraine, and most places in between, Irish missionaries carried the Christian message back to a shattered and demoralized continent. They founded religious settlements both inside and outside the boundaries of the old empire. Germanic and Slav lands beyond the old imperial borders were evangelized.

For instance, the patron saint of Würzburg in northern Bavaria, well outside the empire, is the Irish monk St Killian who evangelized the district in the late seventh century. To the south-west of Würzburg, near the border with Alsace, a small street is named for the saint.

The early Irish Church was monastic because there were no towns in Gaelic Ireland, as there were on the continent. That meant that continental Christianity developed a diocesan and parish structure, whereas the monasteries were the nearest equivalent in

Ireland. They have sometimes been seen as proto-towns, but this is fanciful. There are no towns in any proper meaning of the word prior to the arrival of the Vikings in the late eighth century.

As continental Christianity recovered, the monastic pattern in Ireland came to seem ever more out of step. Church reform thus followed hot on the heels of the Normans, who had established themselves by the early thirteenth century. In fact, a reform movement had been in train before the arrival of the Normans, with the first bishop of Dublin being consecrated in 1074. But the Normans accelerated the redirection of the early Irish Church towards Rome.

That said, some abuses appear to have persisted right up to the Reformation. Customary Irish law on marriage and sexuality generally were out of line with orthodox Christian teaching. As late as 1500, we learn of a lady in what is now Co. Cavan, herself the daughter of a bishop, who married the son of a priest who had at least twelve more children. Despite this, he was held to be 'a gem of purity and a turtle dove of chastity', admittedly in a book of which he himself was part author.

The Reformation

The Reformation of western Christianity tripped off by Martin Luther in 1517 was the great ideological battleground of the age. Everything that has happened in Ireland since has been coloured by it. The reason is simple.

England, Scotland and Wales all accepted some version of Protestantism. Most of Ireland did not. Ireland, with the exception of Ulster, remained Catholic. Even in Ulster, where Protestantism established itself it was by dispossession and plantation. In the rest of the British Isles, it was by conviction.

It meant that Ireland, a sister kingdom of the English crown, opted out of the Reformation settlement – or at least most of it did. That was bad enough, in an age when religious affiliation really mattered. Being a Catholic in a largely Protestant environment was rather like being an American communist during the Cold War. Catholics could not be trusted, with good reason.

There were Catholic plots against Queen Elizabeth's life. The papacy was her declared enemy. Rome did not finally acknowledge the legitimacy of British Protestant monarchs until 1766, almost 250 years after Luther had posted his 95 theses to the door of the Castle Church in Wittenberg.

As a largely Catholic island lying astride the western seaborne approaches to Britain, Ireland was to be a constant source of anxiety for London, which feared that it might be used as an invasion beachhead by Catholic continental powers – first Spain and later France. And indeed such efforts were made from time to time over the years.

What was worse was the fatal division within Ireland itself, specifically in Ulster. It is hardly necessary to spell it out again. The consequences are with us to this day. The divisions in Ulster are not the cause of a religious war, but religious affiliation is the most visible outward sign of the tribal divide.

Roman Catholicism

Formally, Roman Catholics (RCs) constitute the overwhelming majority in ROI and a substantial and growing minority in NI. Latest census figures suggest that about 80 per cent of people in ROI declare themselves as RCs but the methodology producing these estimates has been challenged. What may be stated with conviction is that (a) this number is not overstated and (b) that the longer-term trend is one of decline. In Northern Ireland, the RC minority has now passed 40 per cent of the total population.

The RC church is organized on an all-Ireland basis:

ECCLESIASTICAL PROVINCES: Armagh, Dublin, Cashel, Tuam (roughly corresponding to the four geographical provinces).

DIOCESES (ARMAGH)

Armagh, archdiocese
Ardagh and Clonmacnoise
Clogher
Derry
Down and Connor
Dromore
Kilmore
Meath
Raphoe

DIOCESES (DUBLIN)

Dublin, archdiocese
Ferns
Kildare and Leighlin
Ossory

DIOCESES (CASHEL)

Cashel and Emly, archdiocese
Cloyne
Cork and Ross
Kerry
Killaloe
Limerick
Waterford and Lismore

DIOCESES (TUAM)

Tuam, archdiocese
Achonry
Clonfert
Elphin
Galway, Kilmacduagh and Kilfenora
Killala

Anglicanism

In ROI, the most recent census figures indicate that the Church of Ireland claims the allegiance of 5 per cent of the population. The equivalent figure for NI is about 14 per cent, which represents about 65 per cent of all Irish Anglicans.

The organization of the Church of Ireland echoes that of the Roman Catholic Church on a smaller scale, as follows:

There are only two provinces, Armagh and Dublin, roughly dividing the island in half north and south.

DIOCESES (ARMAGH)

Armagh, archdiocese
Clogher
Connor
Derry and Raphoe
Down and Dromore
Kilmore, Elphin and Ardagh
Tuam, Killala and Achonry

DIOCESES (DUBLIN)

Dublin, archdiocese
Cashel and Ossory
Cork, Cloyne and Ross
Limerick and Killaloe
Meath and Kildare

Presbyterianism

The Presbyterian Church in Ireland is overwhelmingly concentrated in NI, where it is the largest Protestant denomination, being about

19 per cent of the province's population. The equivalent figure for ROI is 2 per cent.

As a Calvinist church, it does not have bishops and therefore has no diocesan structure. Its headquarters are in Belfast. Its principal governing body is the General Assembly, which annually elects a member of the clergy as its Moderator. It has, therefore, the most democratic governing institutions of all the major Christian denominations.

This emphasis on democratic governance and the primacy of personal judgement over imposed or suggested authority has led to many theological controversies over the centuries and also to splits. In the modern era, the most dramatic and significant of these was the creation of the Free Presbyterian Church, founded in 1951 by the charismatic Rev. Ian Paisley, who ended his career as First Minister of Northern Ireland and who preached an uncompromising and fundamentalist version of the reformed faith.

Huguenots

Some further efforts at Protestant plantation in Ireland were more successful than others. The most significant group, the Huguenots, were French Calvinists. Their toleration and legal protections by the French crown were withdrawn in 1685, in a mirror image of anti-Catholic intolerance in England. Many took refuge in England but some made it all the way to Ireland.

There, they settled in the area of Dublin known as the Liberties – near St Patrick's Cathedral – and introduced the weaving industry, in which they were highly skilled, to the city. Weaver's Street in that area is a reminder of their presence.

The Huguenots were also involved in banking. In the eighteenth century, the La Touche family were an important presence in the Irish financial world. The Le Fanu family likewise produced people of distinction: Joseph Sheridan Le Fanu (1814–73) was the author of dark Gothic fiction and an influence on later Irish writers.

The most permanent mark left by the Huguenots was in Ulster, where they settled in Lurgan, near Belfast. The key figure here was one Samuel-Louis Crommelin, who came to Ireland at the express invitation of King William III, who offered him the post of 'overseer of the royal linen manufacture of Ireland'. Crommelin and his fellow-Huguenots brought the most advanced continental manufacturing techniques with them, in an echo of what their co-religionists were bringing to the weaving trade in Dublin.

A Linen Board was established in Dublin in 1711, to give grants to the industry and lobby parliament in its interests. But linen manufacture was heavily concentrated in east Ulster and in time it seemed to make more sense to trade the finished product through Belfast rather than Dublin. Thus was built in Belfast the White Linen Hall on the site of the present City Hall. It was another small marker of Ulster particularism, bypassing Dublin.

In the days of Belfast's pomp – the late nineteenth century up to World War I – its leading department store was known formally as the Royal Irish Linen Warehouse, although universally known by the name of its founders, Robinson & Cleaver. Linen was its stock-in-trade and some estimates reckoned that a third of all the parcels sent overseas from Belfast originated in this one shop. It closed in 1984, in the depths of the troubles, although the beautiful *Jugendstil* building still stands on the corner of Donegall Square and Donegall Place.

Palatines

The Palatines were Protestant refugees from the Rhineland Palatinate, which had been devastated by French troops in the wars of the 1690s. They came to Ireland and were settled in a number of the southern counties. In all, they numbered only about 3,000 persons. They discovered that their new Anglican landlords displayed a limited tolerance for their passionate Calvinism. By the end of the eighteenth century, many Palatines had emigrated to the United States.

Yet those that remained left their mark. Veronica Guerin – her surname originally a Palatine one – was a celebrated investigative journalist in Dublin who was murdered by gangsters in 1996. Her death caused a huge political furore around organized crime and she was commemorated in two feature films.

One of Dublin's leading department stores for much of the twentieth century was Switzer's, named for its founder, John Wright Switzer, who was descended from a Palatine family in Co. Tipperary.

Faith and Fatherland

One effect of the Reformation was to emphasize Catholicism as the principal marker of Irish difference. It was further marked by the land confiscations in which Catholic landowners were replaced by English Anglicans. This was ever after regarded as illegitimate.

It is hardly surprising, in this context, that Catholic grievances gradually morphed into something more substantial. Once the French Revolution had introduced nationalist ideas to Europe, the Catholic question in Ireland quickly became the national question.

Was it inevitable? It seems so in retrospect. There was a genuine and sincere attempt in the 1790s to propose an Irish nationalism that was purely secular and non-sectarian. But there were always tensions, even then. Many Ulster Presbyterians, who felt oppressed by Anglican landlords, were republicans while harbouring doubts about Roman Catholic commitment to such enlightened beliefs.

The rising of 1798 settled the question. For all the professed secularism of Wolfe Tone and others, the rebellion in Co. Wexford soon showed a sectarian side. The massacre of more than a hundred Protestants near New Ross was only the most conspicuous example of the sectarian outrages. Overall, 1798 effectively ended Presbyterian and liberal Anglican flirtations with non-sectarian nationalism.

When Irish nationalism got going in earnest in the 1820s under

Daniel O'Connell, it was on a specifically Catholic demand. The achievement of Catholic Emancipation in 1829 was the high-water mark of O'Connell's career. He had appealed quite openly to the union of faith and fatherland, a concept that was familiar to his audiences: it had been around in one form or another since the 1640s. Now, almost 200 years later, it was front and centre of Irish life and there it stayed.

Irish Catholic nationalism eventually detached 26 of the island's 32 counties from the union with Britain. The attempt to secure the remaining six failed precisely because what became Northern Ireland had a non-Catholic majority. Everyone, regardless of affiliation, understood this simple calculus: Catholic equalled nationalist, Protestant equalled unionist. The few exceptions to the rule were statistically insignificant.

The Catholic Church in the South retained a position of extra-ordinary influence, described by one writer as a moral monopoly as late as the 1980s. In 1986, as we have seen (see p. 202) church influence saw the decisive defeat of a proposal to introduce divorce. Ten years later, a similar proposal was carried – if only just.

What had changed? More than anything, an advancing sec-ularism was swept along by a series of clerical sex abuse scandals which broke the moral monopoly and weakened the automatic link between faith and fatherland, although it remained stronger among nationalists in Northern Ireland.

JEWS

The small Jewish community in Ireland is principally descended from Ashkenazi Jews fleeing from persecution in the Russian Pale of Settlement – Lithuania in particular – in the late nineteenth century. The community has always been small – never more than 5,000 people – and it was concentrated mainly in an area in the south inner city of Dublin popularly referred to as Little Jerusalem. Small communities also established themselves in Belfast, Cork and Limerick.

Leopold Bloom, the fictional hero of Joyce's *Ulysses*, lived for a while in Lombard Street West in the heart of Little Jerusalem, although he is across the river in Eccles Street by the time we make his acquaintance.

There had been a tiny Jewish presence in Ireland, probably numbered in the hundreds rather than the thousands, before the late nineteenth-century influx. There is a Jewish burial ground in the north Dublin suburb of Ballybough (*Baile Bocht*: poor town) bearing the Hebraic date 5618, otherwise 1858.

The most serious case of Irish anti-Semitism occurred in Limerick in 1904. A Redemptorist priest preached a sermon against the local Jewish community and instigated a boycott of Jewish businesses. This drew some short-term local support but was vigorously opposed by many figures prominent in Irish public life. The boycott ended after about two weeks; some Jewish families left Limerick, although others remained. This ugly incident was unique.

The modern community is tiny. Emigration to larger Jewish communities in the UK and the United States – as well as to Israel – has depleted the Jewish presence in Irish life.

Despite their small numbers, members of the Irish Jewish community have made a significant contribution to the nation's life. Here are some of the more prominent:

Chaim Herzog, born Belfast, educated Dublin, sixth
    President of Israel
Harry Kernoff, artist
Estella Solomons, artist and patriot
Bethel Solomons, medical doctor and rugby international
Robert Briscoe, republican and twice Lord Mayor of Dublin
Gerald Goldberg, Lord Mayor of Cork
David Marcus, writer, editor, patron of writers
Louis Marcus, film-maker
Mervyn Taylor, cabinet minister
Alan Shatter, cabinet minister
Lenny Abrahamson, film-maker

That list could be twice as long again. It has been an astonishing contribution to Irish national life from a community with such exiguous numbers. To it could be added the names of distinguished lawyers, academics, journalists and sportsmen. The decline in Jewish numbers is one of the saddest features of contemporary Ireland.

MUSLIMS

The number professing the Islamic faith has grown dramatically in modern times. In 1991 there were fewer than 4,000 in ROI; by 2015, it was estimated that this number had increased to more than 63,000. The community is overwhelmingly Sunni.

15

EDUCATION

There were few schools in Ireland prior to the eighteenth century. A small number, such as Kilkenny College where Jonathan Swift was educated, were of earlier foundation. There were also some private academies, such as White's in Dublin and Abraham Shackleton's Quaker School in Co. Kildare, which was attended by Edmund Burke. The basic purpose of these institutions was to prepare the tiny elite who received any kind of education for entry to Trinity College.

A complicating factor was the disruption caused by the Reformation and its aftermath. It entailed the effective dismantling of such systems of Catholic instruction as existed. The consequence of this was the establishment of a network of Irish Colleges in Catholic Europe, mainly for the training of elite Irish clergy as the foot soldiers of the Counter-Reformation.

The earliest of these was in Salamanca (1592). In all, the network grew to more than thirty. Among the best known were the ones at Leuven, Paris, Rome and Lisbon. The relaxation of the Penal Laws in the eighteenth century, combined with the upheavals of the French Revolution and the opening of the Irish national seminary at Maynooth in 1795 brought a gradual end to this continental tradition.

In addition, privileged Irish Catholic laymen sought their education in Europe – as did upper-class English recusants. Many went to one of the colleges in the network just noted. Others, such as Daniel O'Connell, went to separate establishments – in his case the Jesuit school in St Omer.

In the course of the nineteenth century, systems of education were developed at primary, secondary and tertiary levels. These were consolidated under formal state control after partition in the 1920s, although the churches retained a substantial influence in the sector.

Primary

The first system of national primary education was established in 1831 by E.G. Stanley, later Earl of Derby, the Chief Secretary for Ireland (the political head of Irish affairs under the Act of Union). It was intended to be strictly non-denominational, even to the extent of excluding priests and ministers from teaching posts.

All the major churches set aside their considerable differences to unite against this measure. By the end of the 1830s, the system was mutating into an increasingly sectarian pattern. Influential Catholic teaching orders, such as the Christian Brothers (established 1802) and the Presentation Order (1776), withdrew from the system.

The Christian Brothers became the most influential of all the Catholic teaching orders. They offered an education to lower-middle-class boys whose parents could not afford the fee-paying schools run by other religious orders. Their system was strictly utilitarian, focused very much on success in state examinations, nationalist in its ethos and culture and at times ferocious in its discipline.

Teacher training colleges, once more divided along confessional lines, developed from the 1880s. By the early twentieth century, the spread of the primary school system had ensured a near universal competence in basic literacy and numeracy but progression to secondary level was still reserved for a minority.

Until the education reforms of the twentieth century, this inequality persisted. In ROI, as late as the early 1960s, only 28 per cent of primary pupils had passed the national certificate examination that completed the cycle; 18 per cent had failed or been absent; no less than 54 per cent could not be traced at all!

In recent decades, two related developments have been notable in the ROI system. A multi-denominational school network has grown which is independent of the churches and is parent controlled. The first such school opened in Dublin in 1978 and an umbrella body for the sector dates from 1984. The growth of multi-denominational education has mirrored the decline in the fortunes of the Catholic Church and the continuing secularization of Irish society, especially among the urban middle class.

The other interesting development is the growth of the Gaelscoileanna, schools whose medium of instruction is the Irish language. As with the multi-denominational sector, the Gaelscoileanna are independent of clerical control and subject to democratic parent governance. There are almost 200 such schools scattered throughout the country, all of them located in English-speaking areas. As with the multi-denominational schools, it is hard not to see further expansion in the future.

Secondary

At elite level, a network of boys' Catholic schools had been developed during the nineteenth century. The two most significant religious orders in this regard were the Society of Jesus – the Jesuits – and the Holy Ghost Order. When the Jesuits opened Clongowes Wood College in Co. Kildare in 1814, it was the first such school launched in Ireland since the Reformation. The Holy Ghosts were a French missionary order: they brought with them a tradition of hostility to the French Revolution that helped to shape the conservative disposition of the emerging Catholic and nationalist elite.

Further down the social scale, the Christian Brothers and other orders such as the De La Salle Brothers offered a secondary education on a no fee or minimal fee basis. None the less, the numbers in the ROI system remained very low until the 1960s.

In NI, secondary education did not open up to poorer families – disproportionately Catholics – until the UK Education Act of 1944 transformed the situation, offering the prospect of free secondary education for all. In ROI, free secondary education did not come until 1967. At the start of the 1960s, ROI was almost alone among Western European countries in its disregard for equal educational opportunity.

For example, until the introduction of the free scheme, barely one in three children received some sort of secondary education; the equivalent figure for (West) Germany was four in five. Moreover, the curriculum had a grossly classical bias, as noted in an OECD report in 1963. Less than one secondary school in six in ROI taught chemistry to the end of the secondary cycle. Only 10 per cent of boys took science at all; unsurprisingly, the figure for girls was even lower.

In ROI, a system of vocational and technical education was developed, aimed principally at apprenticeship training for various trades. It lacked the cachet of the secondary system, into which it was largely absorbed following the 1960s reforms.

Those reforms were probably the single most successful achievement of the independent Irish state. In 1966, a scheme of free second-level education open to all was announced, together with free transport provision for pupils living three miles or more from their nearest school. The effect was dramatic. When the free scheme was introduced, fewer than 20 per cent of pupils completed the secondary cycle all the way to the Leaving Certificate. A mere thirty years later, in the mid-1990s, the equivalent figure was over 80 per cent.

Most secondary schools in ROI bought into the free scheme, although a minority declined and continued to charge fees. The huge expansion of second-level education in turn caused an increase in third-level participation. Overall, the effect has been to produce a well-educated, skilled young workforce which, combined with a favourable demographic, proved attractive to foreign companies establishing themselves in Ireland in the so-called Celtic Tiger years. It was not the only consideration – access to EU markets, an anglophone environment and a very low rate of corporation tax were hardly immaterial – but it was significant.

The education system in NI differs from the rest of the UK in one crucial respect: selection. In the rest of the UK, the old Eleven Plus examination, which decided whether eleven-year-olds were destined to take their second-level education at desirable grammar schools or undesirable secondary moderns was abolished in the

1960s in favour of an across-the-board comprehensive system. NI retained selection and has consistently produced the highest exam grades in the UK.

Although the Eleven Plus has now been abolished in NI, individual schools still practise an informal system of selection. The schools themselves are mostly divided along confessional lines. State schools are Protestant, while Catholic schools are independently maintained.

A movement for integrated schools has heroically promoted its cause, even through the darkest years of the troubles. It has had little to show for its effort. Barely 5 per cent of NI pupils attend such schools.

Third Level

Until 1845, there was just one university in what is now ROI. That is Trinity, the only constituent college of the University of Dublin. It dates from 1592 and was founded as 'the college of the holy and undivided Trinity' for the purpose of inculcating 'civilitie, learning and true religion'.

In 1845, a number of secular Queen's Colleges were established, in Belfast, Cork and Galway. Queen's University Belfast retains (almost) its original name. The other two are respectively the antecedents of University College Cork (UCC) and the National University of Ireland Galway (NUIG).

This did not satisfy the demands for a specifically Catholic university, by nationalists effectively seeking to create a rival to Protestant Trinity. The Queen's Colleges were noisily denounced as 'godless college'. A Catholic University was indeed established in Dublin in 1854 with episcopal support; its first rector was John Henry Newman. It went through a number of evolutions and name changes, eventually to emerge as University College Dublin (UCD), now the largest institution of higher learning in Ireland.

No further development of the university system occurred until the second half of the twentieth century. Then, in step with the rest of the developed world and arising naturally out of the educational expansion at second level, the sector flourished.

In 1972 a National Institute for Higher Education was established in Limerick, with a similar institute opening in Dublin three years later. These were technical colleges along the models long established in Germany, aiming to complement what were still considered the excessive liberal arts bias in the older universities. In 1989, they acquired full university status, as the University of Limerick and Dublin City University. Student numbers in both institutions are about 13,000.

The National University of Ireland Maynooth – just to the west of Dublin – is a historical hybrid. It has evolved out of the national Catholic seminary which dates to 1795 and still maintains a residual existence, despite the huge decline in vocations. Its current status, independent of the pontifical college although sharing the same campus, dates from 1997. It has over 8,000 students.

In NI, Queen's was the only third-level institution until the opening of the University of Ulster in 1968. Now simply called Ulster University, it has incorporated a number of other colleges as well as its original campus at Coleraine, Co. Derry. Student numbers are about 22,000. The Open University also has a presence in NI, with over 5,000 students from the province registered.

In addition to the universities, there are Institutes of Technology and Colleges of Education in every part of the country. Some specialist colleges are long established and have international reputations, such as the Royal College of Surgeons in Ireland (1784) and the Royal College of Physicians in Ireland (1654). The Royal Irish Academy (1785) is a centre of post-doctoral multidisciplinary research.

In 1940, Éamon de Valera was instrumental in establishing the Dublin Institute for Advanced Studies. It does not award degrees but trains students in advanced research. There are three schools in the Institute: Theoretical Physics, Cosmic Physics and Celtic Studies. The first director of the School of Theoretical Physics was the internationally renowned Erwin Schrödinger. His suggestion that it was impossible to propose a 'first cause' of the world's existence, combined with another scholar in the School of Celtic Studies speculating that there had been more than one national evangelist, led Myles na gCopaleen, writing his satirical column in the *Irish Times* to lampoon the Institute thus:

> I understand also that Professor Schrödinger has been proving lately that you cannot establish a first cause. The first fruit of the Institute therefore, has been an effort to show that there are two Saint Patricks and no God.

In addition to all the publicly funded universities, colleges, institutes and teacher-training facilities, there are numerous private colleges usually specializing in courses directed at business and commerce students, with a firm emphasis on professional vocational training. A number of language schools, especially in the Dublin area, reflect Ireland's popularity as a destination for persons learning English.

Taking the traffic in the other direction, Dublin hosts offices of the major European cultural institutes: the Alliance Française, the Goethe-Institut, the Instituto Cervantes and the Istituto Italiana di Cultura.

16

ARMY, NAVY AND POLICE

The Defence Forces of the ROI comprise

- Permanent Defence Force (9,500 personnel)
- Reserve Defence Force

The Permanent Defence Force comprises

- Army
- Naval Service
- Air Corps

The Army contains two brigades, based in Dublin and Cork. The Naval Service is based at Haulbowline, Co. Cork and the Air Corps at Baldonnel near Dublin.

The Army operates on a system of voluntary enlistment: there is no conscription. Its primary purpose is to defend the state against invasion or other forms of armed aggression, including – as required from time to time – armed subversion from within by illegal or proscribed militias. In a more general context, it aids the civil power as circumstances dictate on the instructions of the government.

The Army also has a proud record of service in support of the United Nations' security missions. Ireland joined the UN in 1955. Since then, the Army has seen service under UN mandates in the following territories:

Congo	1960–64
Cyprus	1964–
Lebanon	1978–2001
Iran–Iraq	1988–91
Somalia	1993–
Bosnia–Herzegovina	1995–
East Timor	1999–
Kosovo	1999–

The Army comprises nine corps:

Infantry	Medical

Artillery	Military Police
Cavalry	Ordnance
Engineers	Transport & Vehicle
Communications and	Maintenance
Information	

The remote origins of the army lay in the formation of the Irish Volunteers in 1913, as a militia to support the political demand for home rule. It was founded in response to the Ulster Volunteers, a unionist militia in Ulster which opposed home rule. After the Easter Rising of 1916 and the War of Independence (1919–21), the nationalist movement split over the terms of the Anglo-Irish Treaty, leading to the short but intense civil war of 1922–23. The National Army was formed to defend the settlement and from it grew the modern Irish army.

The Naval Service dates from 1946. Prior to that, independent Ireland had no naval force until the start of World War II in 1939. Then a Marine Service was formed to patrol the Irish coast; the Naval Service is its successor.

Its principal duty is fishing protection in Ireland's exclusive territorial waters, which cover 200 nautical miles from the coast. The service is possessed of eight ships; its personnel is just over 1,000. It also assists the civil power as required, in particular helping to prevent and detect drug smuggling.

The Air Corps was founded in 1924 and for many years was part of the army, only becoming an autonomous branch of the Defence Forces in the 1990s. It comprises 24 aircraft and about 700 personnel. It is basically a support service for the army and navy, as well as performing such civilian duties as providing an emergency air ambulance service as required.

The Garda Síochána (Guardians of the Peace), the national police force in ROI, was founded in 1922. Despite the fact that the Civil War was still raging, the remarkable decision was made that the new force should be unarmed and should depend on its moral authority and the legitimacy of the new state for its standing with the public.

It replaced two forces that had operated under British rule, the unarmed Dublin Metropolitan Police (DMP) and the Royal Irish Constabulary (RIC). The RIC had been an armed force operating everywhere outside the capital, making it even more of a novelty that the Gardaí were unarmed.

Although a national force, it is based on six regions, each under the command of an Assistant Commissioner. These regions in turn are broken down into divisions under the direction of a Chief Superintendent. As of January 2017, the force had the following establishment:

Commissioner	1
Deputy Commissioner	2
Assistant Commissioners	8
Chief Superintendents	44
Superintendents	165
Inspectors	307
Sergeants	1,936
Gardaí	10,460
Subtotal	**12,923**
Civilians	1,996
Total	**14,919**
Garda Reserve	690

Source: Garda Press Office

While most Gardaí remain unarmed, the twin pressures of the NI troubles and the rise of armed organized crime in ROI since the 1980s – the two phenomena are not unconnected – have led to the formation of a number of armed units, the best known of which is the Emergency Response Unit (ERU). Another unit with a high public profile is the Criminal Assets Bureau, formed to investigate and confiscate the earnings of convicted criminals.

The Scott Medal for Bravery is awarded to individual Gardaí for acts of conspicuous courage. The decision to make an award is taken by the Garda Commissioner.

Northern Ireland

As part of the UK, the British Army represents the armed forces of the sovereign power.

Given the communal divisions in NI, the legitimacy of the army is not accepted by many nationalists. Since the end of the troubles, the army has not been a visible presence on the streets. The police, on the other hand, are of necessity visible.

There have been two police forces in the history of NI. First, there was the Royal Ulster Constabulary (RUC), a direct provincial successor to the old RIC. Like the RIC, it was an armed force. It was supported by an armed militia formally known as the Ulster Special Constabulary but universally referred to as the B Specials. Formed in 1921, the RUC was disbanded in 2001 in the wake of the Belfast Agreement of 1998, the breakthrough that led eventually to the settlement of the troubles. It was replaced by the present police body, the Police Service of Northern Ireland (PSNI).

The B Specials were disbanded in 1970 under the pressure of the early troubles. It had long been regarded, with justice, as bigoted and partisan, little more than a loyalist militia. It was replaced as a police reserve by the new Ulster Defence Regiment (UDR). Crucially, the UDR was part of the British army and is under its control.

At the time of writing, the security situation in NI has been thrown into doubt by the UK decision to secede from the EU. This decision, depending on how it is actually implemented, could mean the reinstatement of a 'hard border' with ROI, thus reviving the system of oppressive border controls and the associated security anxieties which were thought to have been happily consigned to history.

17

THE PUBLIC SPHERE

Financial Institutions

The three largest banking groups in Ireland are the Bank of Ireland Group (BOI), Allied Irish Banks (AIB) and Ulster Bank, a subsidiary of the UK's Royal Bank of Scotland (RBS).

BOI was formed from three existing banks, as follows, with foundation dates:

Bank of Ireland	1783
Hibernian Bank	1825
National Bank	1835

The old Bank of Ireland acquired the Hibernian in 1958 and added the National in 1965 to form the modern BOI group. In direct response, the remaining independent banks felt the need to consolidate, which they did in 1966 to form AIB. The constituent banks, with their foundation dates, were:

Provincial	1825
Royal	1836
Munster & Leinster	1885

The Munster & Leinster, although the youngest of the constituent banks, was the largest and its culture has been the dominant one in AIB.

In all, there are thirty holders of banking licences in ROI. Many are specialist services, with the big three having the majority of business in the retail banking sector.

Savings banks were first established in Cork in 1817 and in Dublin the following year. The Post Office Savings Bank was set up in 1861. Building societies appeared from the 1860s onward. They were mutual societies owned by their depositors and not by third-party shareholders. This situation persisted until the move to demutualize building societies in the 1990s led to their conversion into banks or – effectively the same thing – their acquisition by existing banks.

The Irish banking system is subject to the control of the Central Bank of Ireland. Prior to 2010 the Central Bank and the Financial Regulator were separate entities. The backwash from the crash of 2008 led to severe criticism of the performance of the Financial Regulator, leading to the merging of functions. As ROI is a member of the Eurozone, interest rates are determined by the European Central Bank (ECB) in Frankfurt.

The International Financial Services Centre (IFSC) was established in the late 1980s on the north quays of the Liffey in Dublin, offering tax concessions to companies which established a presence there. It has been a success and has revitalized what had been a run-down and shabby part of the city. It has also acquired a reputation as the 'Wild West' of international finance, with a number of businesses there which were mere brass-plate operations, taking advantage of the tax concessions available while the substance of their operations was elsewhere.

The three big banks in ROI also operate in NI, where AIB trades under the name of First Trust Bank. Danske Bank has taken over the NI business of the old Northern Bank but it no longer has branches in ROI.

Media and Communications

TELEVISION

The national broadcaster in ROI is Radio Telefís Éireann (RTÉ), established on a model copied from the BBC, although unlike the BBC it carries commercial advertisements to supplement the revenues raised by the licence fee charged to all households that possess a television set. Advertising accounts for the majority of RTÉ's revenues. The amount of the licence fee is determined by the government.

RTÉ's remit is a broad public-service one. It is governed by the RTÉ Authority, a board of directors appointed by the government.

Each authority sits for five years. In turn, it appoints the Director-General, who is in effect both CEO and editor-in-chief.

It hosts two television channels, RTÉ1 and RTÉ2, the latter being the more commercial of the two.

TV3 is an independent commercial channel financed entirely by advertising and is the principal rival to the RTÉ channels. TG4 is a publicly funded Irish-language service with a strong public-service ethos.

All the major British channels are freely available in ROI.

In NI, the regional channel in the overall UK Independent network is UTV, which is also available in ROI.

RADIO

As with television, radio in ROI is dominated by RTÉ. It hosts four stations: RTÉ Radio 1, which discharges the principal public-service remit; RTÉ 2FM, a popular music station; RTÉ Lyric FM, a classical music station; and RTÉ Raidió na Gaeltachta, an Irish-language station.

The two principal rivals to RTÉ radio are Today FM and Newstalk, the former principally a music station and the latter, as the name suggests, a news and current affairs station.

In addition, there is a large number of independent music stations, most broadcasting locally rather than nationally. Similarly, local and regional radio stations, with an editorial mix of local news and comment, sport and music, are well established.

PRESS

There are three daily newspapers published in ROI, as follows (with foundation dates and circulation figures to June 2016, sourced from the Audit Bureau of Circulations):

Irish Independent (1905)	102,537
Irish Times (1859)	66,251
Irish Examiner (1841)	30,964

The Irish Examiner was formerly the Cork Examiner and its principal sales area is in Munster, although it is classified as a national.

A sister paper of the *Irish Independent*, the *Herald*, is published each afternoon and has sales of 44,085.

There are three Irish-published national Sunday papers, the *Sunday Independent*, whose sales of 199,210 make it by far the top-selling paper in the country; the *Sunday World*, with sales of 162,938; and the *Sunday Business Post*, which sells 32,162 copies.

In addition, Irish editions of the following UK newspapers are published: *Daily Mail*, *Daily Mirror*, *The Times*, the *Sun* and the *Star*.

In NI, the principal papers are the *News-Letter*, read mainly by unionists; the *Irish News*, its nationalist opposite; and the *Belfast Telegraph*, an evening paper. The *News-Letter*, which was first published in 1737, is the oldest continuously published newspaper in the English-speaking world.

In addition to these national and regional papers, there is a lively local press in both ROI and NI, as well as publications such as the *Irish Farmers Journal*, aimed at targeted vocational or special-interest groups.

As is the case everywhere, the effect of social media and digital content generally has had a negative effect on Irish newspaper sales. The sales graph for nearly all titles has shown a steady if shallow decline in recent years. Digital editions are no compensation for the loss of print sales.

Social and Voluntary Organizations

We have already met the Gaelic Athletic Association (p. 187), the voluntary association with the widest reach in Ireland. This chapter looks at some of the more significant social bodies that play a major role in Irish life.

IRISH FARMERS' ASSOCIATION

Despite the advances made by high tech and Big Pharma businesses in the Irish economy over the last generation, agriculture remains a key part of the overall mix. The IFA is the largest body of its kind in the country, claiming to represent 88,000 farm families. It has 946 branches and maintains an office in Brussels. That last point is telling: Irish agriculture depends on the supports offered by the EU's Common Agricultural Policy. The IFA not only maintains a strong lobbying presence at European level, it is also a potent influence in domestic politics. It represents, for the most part, the interests of the larger farmers. Given the nature of the Irish PR-STV voting system, no political party can remain indifferent to its concerns.

SIPTU

The Services Industrial Professional and Technical Union is the largest trade union in the country. It claims a membership of more than 200,000 and is based in Liberty Hall, a sixteen-storey building of minimal to zero architectural distinction which stands on the north quay of the Liffey. SIPTU is the lineal successor to the Irish Transport and General Workers' Union, founded by the legendary labour leader James Larkin in 1907. It originally focused on mobilizing unskilled workers – offering an alternative to the British-based craft unions which represented skilled tradesmen. Following defeat in the great transport lockout of 1913, Larkin left for the United States. James Connolly took over the ITGWU but was executed for his part in the 1916 Rising. Larkin returned to Ireland in 1923 to form a rival union, the Workers' Union of Ireland. In 1990, the ITGWU and the WUI finally reconciled and reunited to form SIPTU.

CONSTRUCTION INDUSTRY FEDERATION

One of the most potent lobbying groups in the country, representing a critical economic interest. As well as representing the material interests of the construction industry to government, the CIF also provides support services to its members in areas such as training and development, financial advice and public planning. It also concerns itself with industrial relations issues and the reputational profile of the industry. It supports thirty-one specialist associations in specific areas such as civil and electrical engineering contractors, structural steel manufacturing and concrete production.

Aosdána

An academy of creative artists founded with government support in 1981. It acknowledges publicly distinguished achievements in the creative arts. It was regarded as a retrospective apology for the decades of censorship that had been such a prominent feature of the earlier independent Irish state. Membership of Aosdána is determined by peer nomination and election. It offers bursaries to members to relieve financial distress.

Irish Countrywomen's Association

The ICA is the Irish equivalent of the Women's Institute in the UK. Founded in 1910, it quickly established itself as one of the key voluntary bodies in Irish social life. It offered mutual support, educational opportunities and recreational activities at a time when there was still much formal discrimination against women in Irish public life. Its headquarters are in Dublin but it also maintains an adult education college, An Grianán (The Sunny Place) in Termonfeckin, Co. Louth. It has over 10,000 members in all parts of the country. It insists that the word 'country' in the title refers to the nation rather than to anything specifically rural. Indeed, its largest guild is in the west Dublin suburb of Blanchardstown.

Royal Dublin Society

Founded in 1731 as the Dublin Society – the Royal moniker was added in 1820 when King George IV agreed to become a patron – the RDS is an Irish institution. It started as a classic expression of eighteenth-century Enlightenment ambition, aiming to use practical means to support agriculture, industry, science and art in Ireland. In its early years, it relied on private funding but over time it was able to attract government funding which enabled it to develop its holdings and collections. These formed the basis of what later became the National Library, the National Museum and the National College of Art. In addition, the National Botanic Gardens began as an RDS venture. In 1814, the Society bought Leinster House in Dublin from the Duke of Leinster and in the 1870s the buildings that now house the National Library and the National

Museum were erected on its flanks. The RDS moved out of Leinster House in 1880 to its current premises in the suburb of Ballsbridge, where it had far greater exhibition space.

Marsh's Library

This is the oldest public library in Ireland and one of the earliest in the British Isles. It occupies a plain Georgian building beside St Patrick's Cathedral in Dublin. It was built by Archbishop Narcissus Marsh (1638–1713) in 1701 to a design by Sir William Robinson, who also designed the Royal Hospital in Kilmainham, now home to the Irish Museum of Modern Art. Marsh's Library has hardly changed its appearance since it first opened. Its main collection of about 25,000 books relates to the sixteenth, seventeenth and early eighteenth centuries. In addition, it holds about 300 manuscripts. There are three wire 'cages' where readers of rare books were locked in as a security measure.

Orange Order

The Orange Order dates from 1795. It was formed as the result of a sectarian affray in Co. Armagh. It is the largest Protestant organization in Northern Ireland, with a membership of about 100,000 people. Its title refers to King William of Orange (William III), the Protestant monarch who triumphed over the Catholic James II at the time of the Glorious Revolution. Although it sees itself primarily as a fraternal association offering mutual support to its members, it is best known for its annual marches, many of which have been a source of political and social tensions. In particular, marches through areas of Northern Ireland that are predominantly nationalist and Catholic are regarded as provocative coat-trailing. Its main day of celebration is 12 July, commemorating the victory of William over James at the Battle of the Boyne, when marches take place at about twenty venues, the principal one being in Belfast.

18

TEN SUCCESS STORIES

Ryanair

Ryanair is now one of the biggest brands in Europe, but like everything big it was small once. It was born in November 1985 and named for its founder, Tony Ryan. Ryan had made a fortune from his aircraft leasing company, GPA, which he was to lose after a botched market flotation of the company in 1992. But in 1985 he was riding high. His new airline took on Aer Lingus on the key Dublin–London route, with Ryanair offering return flights to Luton for a mere £99, less than half of what Aer Lingus and British Airways were charging.

It didn't work. In under three years, it had accumulated losses of more than £7 million. By 1991, when Michael O'Leary was appointed as deputy chief executive, it seemed a financial basket case. O'Leary himself thought it was beyond rescue and recommended that Ryan close it. Ryan refused. Losses had now reached £22 million but a fierce cost-cutting programme produced an annual surplus of £100,000 that year. The little airline had turned the corner.

It now had one of the lowest, if not the very lowest, cost base of any airline in Europe. Its business model was copied from Southwest Airlines, an American low fares, no frills airline that had been consistently profitable for the best part of thirty years. By 1992, Ryanair was carrying 2.5 million passengers and reporting a profit of £850,000, a figure that many felt was artificially depressed by a very conservative accounting policy. O'Leary stepped up to become chief executive at the end of 1993, by which time the airline was solidly in profit.

From there, it seemed that there was no looking back. Low fares, a rock-bottom cost base, an expanding network and audacious discounts negotiated both for landing charges at airports and for aircraft purchased from Boeing proved an irresistible combination. For many years now, Ryanair has been the largest airline in Europe. But it is more than that. It is one thing to be spectacularly successful, quite another to revolutionize an entire industry.

Wexford Festival Opera

Wexford is a pleasant county town in the south-east of Ireland. It is, however, a most improbable venue for an acclaimed international opera festival, one which attracts audiences from far and near every October. It originally evolved out of a Wexford Opera Study Group, which hosted a lecture in 1950 by Sir Compton Mackenzie who, although best known as a comic novelist, was also a distinguished music critic.

It was Mackenzie who encouraged the enterprise and he became its first president, with the initial festival taking place in 1951. That last point is noteworthy in itself, for the 1950s was perhaps the most dismal decade in modern Irish history – with distressing levels of emigration driven by economic failure. It was not a time when too many international success stories originated anywhere in Ireland.

The moving spirit behind the early festivals was the inaugural artistic director, T.J. Walsh. The Wexford Festival established its distinctive niche on the international opera circuit by staging performances of little-known works or, alternatively, neglected works by major composers. The very first opera given was *The Rose of Castille* by the Irish composer Michael William Balfe (an opera that prompted a lame joke in *Ulysses* when one of the minor characters asks which opera sounds like a railway line: rows of cast steel).

Early festivals featured two operas, and in due time a third was added. That is now the standard. In addition, there is a series of scheduled ancillary musical events around the town – lunchtime concerts, recitals and suchlike – on each of the days.

The Theatre Royal in Wexford was the home of the festival until 2005. It was demolished and a new Wexford Opera House was built on the site, opening in 2008. It increased the capacity of the main auditorium as well as providing a smaller recital room. From its unlikely beginning, the Wexford Festival Opera has long since established itself as a settled favourite on the international opera circuit.

Coolmore Stud

The Irish love of horses and horse racing is long established. But as with most things, especially where large sums of money are in play, it is tough at the top. In the world of thoroughbred breeding, that is exactly where Coolmore Stud is. It is the largest such operation in the world.

The owner and proprietor is John Magnier, who was the son-in-law of Vincent O'Brien, the legendary trainer (see p. 196). O'Brien had previously been co-owner of the property. From the late 1960s, Coolmore began to source thoroughbreds in the North American market. Its earliest successes came from the progeny of a Canadian stallion called Northern Dancer, which itself had had a successful racing career earlier in the decade.

The first exceptional horse sired by Northern Dancer and trained by Vincent O'Brien was Nijinsky, who proved simply to be one of the greatest thoroughbreds of all time. In 1970, Nijinsky won the English Triple Crown – the 2,000 Guineas, the Epsom Derby and the Doncaster St Leger. It was a feat last achieved in 1935 and has not been repeated since. The varying distances of the three races – one mile, a mile and a half and a mile and three-quarters respectively – make immense demands of stamina on the racehorses involved.

Northern Dancer's progeny purchased by Coolmore included The Minstrel, winner of both the Epsom and Irish Derbies in 1977 and El Gran Senor, winner of the 2,000 Guineas and the Irish Derby in 1984. Yet another son of Northern Dancer, Sadler's Wells, won the Irish 2,000 Guineas and the Eclipse Stakes in 1984. More importantly, it in turn sired a series of stallions that had great success both on the track and at stud, with generations of top thoroughbreds being sired at Coolmore.

The operation is now international, with branches in the United States and Australia. As of 2016, there are 45 stallions standing at Coolmore studs internationally, although the majority are in

Ireland. In addition, there are 16 National Hunt sires standing, all in Ireland. It is the most formidable business of its kind anywhere.

Merriman Summer School

Ireland loves its summer schools, where like-minded enthusiasts foregather at an appointed venue – generally well away from Dublin – for four or five days of lectures, networking, conversation and, er, socializing.

The doyen of Irish summer schools is the Yeats in Sligo which dates back to 1960. The Merriman, known colloquially as The Lark in the Clare Air, began in 1967. (The colloquialism is a pun on a nineteenth-century song, 'The Lark in the Clear Air'.) The point about it was that it was supposed to be a one-off.

Brian Merriman, you see, is known only for a single surviving work, a long poem of just over 1,000 lines in Irish entitled 'Cúirt an Mheán Oiche '/ 'The Midnight Court'. He was born and lived in Co. Clare (which is why the school always takes place in that county) from about 1750 to 1805. The poem deals in a comic fashion with questions of love, marriage and sexuality and possesses a degree of bawdy frankness not always associated with Gaelic verse.

The court, which sits at night, is basically an examination of the male world by female inquisitors who, perhaps to no great surprise, find the men wanting. The ostensible theme of the poem proposes a countryside with a large surplus of young women to young men – this is highly improbable in reality; we cannot know with any certainty in a pre-censal age – but reality is not the point. Satire is. Why, the women of the court complain, are there so few men of marriageable age to wed all the available women?

An unmarried poet – probably a surrogate for Merriman himself, who was still unmarried at the age of 30 – is in the dock. Why, the women complain, is this poet denying his love to women who dream of sexual fulfilment? Is he excessively impressed by the celibacy of the clergy? Such marriages as there are may more likely be for money than for love – and often between older men and younger women. What about the fine, lusty young men who should be doing their duty?

Naturally, the defendant gets short shrift in this court. But the poem itself is both witty and bawdy, with more than slight hints of Chaucer and Rabelais. It also touches on the developing puritanism of Irish Catholicism, although Merriman did not live to see the full flowering of this tendency, with all its sexual repression, after 1850. None the less, there are hints of a contemporary anxiety: it is interesting to have matters touching on emotional and sexual wastefulness articulated by women rather than by men.

At all events, this is all we have of Merriman; just this one poem. It stands alone in more senses than one. So, what was a summer school devoted to this singular work expected to be? Singular. There would only be one – a kind of comic reproach to the endless reiterations of the Yeats School up in Sligo. After all, there could only be one. You can no more get blood from the proverbial stone than you can get an endless succession of summer schools from such an exiguous *oeuvre*.

It is still going. And, moreover, they have conjured up a winter school as well. How? Well, the simplest thing was to use Merriman as the loosest possible point of reference for persons of a jolly literary disposition to foregather. The first outing proved so much fun that it seemed a shame not to keep it going. Like minds met like. It was a lot of fun. And, of course, there was the question of the Irish language, scholarly enthusiasts for which were drawn to the school in disproportionate numbers from the start.

Indeed, the organizing society which hosts the school(s) is entitled Cumann Merriman, not the Merriman Society. The combination of the language, a good extended joke, a genuine dedication to discussion, dispute, debate and drink and ingenious editorial themes renewed year on year since 1967 have sealed the Merriman's success. The Lark in the Clare Air is now part of the Irish summer fabric.

The 2016 theme was 'Gallant Allies in Europe', a phrase taken from the 1916 Proclamation of the Republic, whose reference to the

Germans, with whom the United Kingdom was then locked in a war to the death, resonated beyond that original context and had contemporary reverberations in the wake of the economic collapse following the 2008 crash and the sometimes strained relations between Ireland and the European Union institutions that have obtained in the intervening years.

All a long way from Brian Merriman, perhaps. But it is an expression – just one of many – of much that is best in modern Ireland: a determination to have some serious fun, to engage in a public examination and dissection of literary, social and cultural matters that affect all our lives. There are many other such schools: the MacGill in Co. Donegal for the political nerds, the Parnell in Co. Wicklow for the historians, and so on. But the Merriman, although not the most venerable of these (albeit older than the two mentioned), has somehow set the tone for most of the rest.

The fun bit is well attested by all who have ever attended. It is perhaps best expressed by a notice seen in a bed-and-breakfast establishment during one of the Merriman schools, which stated baldly, with a rhetoric that perhaps only an exasperated and put-upon landlady could muster, that Under No Circumstances Will Breakfast Be Served After Lunch. That's the spirit.

Druid

Druid is a theatre company based in Galway. When it was founded in 1975, it was the first professional company in the Republic outside Dublin. Its founders were Garry Hynes – who has remained its leading director and moving spirit – and the actors Mick Lally (died 2010) and Marie Mullen. They first met as students in University College Galway (as it then was) and the company was formed after Lally agreed to give up his career as a history teacher and commit to the theatre. With a brief hiatus in the early 1990s, Hynes has been the company's artistic director from the start.

From its base in the centre of Galway, it has toured all over Ireland

and internationally. It has performed in London and Edinburgh as well as in Australia, New Zealand, the United States, Canada and Japan. All new productions are first presented in Galway.

Its early commitment was to a mixture of international classics, original drama and a broad Irish repertoire. Over time, the Irish element has received most emphasis in its programming. Its earliest success was its landmark production of John Millington Synge's classic comedy *The Playboy of the Western World* in 1982, which was even brought to the Aran Islands in Galway Bay. Its first overseas impact had been at the Edinburgh Fringe Festival in 1980.

The key development for Druid in the 1980s was its association with the work of the Co. Galway born playwright Tom Murphy, an association that seemed to grow organically from the centrality of Synge's plays to the company's early work. Murphy's key play, *Bailegangaire* (the town without laughter) saw the last starring role of the great Irish actor Siobhán McKenna, who played the part of Mommo.

Mommo is a remarkable characterization, senile and rough-tongued as she tells her grandchildren of a laughing competition that ended in tragedy long ago, thus giving the town its subsequent name. The plot is cross-cut with contemporary social concerns, so that in sum it is often regarded as an allegory of Ireland in the 1980s. In all, Druid went on to produce four of Tom Murphy's plays in what was both a key development for the company and one of the most fruitful company–playwright collaborations in modern Irish theatre.

Another such collaboration was that with the London-Irish playwright Martin McDonagh, whose Leenane Trilogy added to the company's burgeoning reputation both in Ireland and internationally. The first of the three plays, *The Beauty Queen of Leenane*, opened in 1996 in a co-production with the Royal Court Theatre in London, a significant new departure for Druid. *A Skull in Connemara* and *The Lonesome West* were staged in 1997 to complete the trilogy. These productions won Tony Awards in New York.

In 2005, at the Galway Arts Festival, Druid produced all six of Synge's plays in a single day, a feat of endurance as well as of artistic triumph. DruidSynge, as it was called, received widespread critical acclaim. One critic, writing in the *New York Times*, said simply: 'It was a highlight not just of my theatregoing year but of my theatregoing life'.

Riverdance

The Eurovision Song Contest has been the launch pad for a few internationally successful acts over the years, of whom Abba are the best known. They won the 1974 contest and went on from there to international stardom and celebrity. It is one thing for a singer or a group to develop into an international phenomenon. It is quite another thing for the interval act in the contest – essentially a filler which generally promotes some aspect of the host country – to follow suit.

Yet that is what *Riverdance* has done. Ireland was the host country for the Eurovision in 1994, with the national broadcaster RTÉ in charge of production. The director was Moya Doherty. She commissioned a piece that would fill the seven-minute interval slot based on an Irish dance routine.

Music was by Bill Whelan with choral backing by Anúna, an ensemble whose repertoire combined medieval and modern Irish music. The choreographer was Michael Flatley, an Irish-American who had trained as an Irish dancer at the Dennis Dennehy School in Chicago. He was little known outside the relatively narrow world of Irish dance; in seven minutes, however, he became a star.

He was the principal performer of *Riverdance*, along with his partner Jean Butler. The performance was mesmerizing – Irish dance crossed with Broadway. The live audience gave it an ecstatic reception. While Ireland won the contest itself – Paul Harrington and Charlie McGettigan's 'Rock 'n' Roll Kids' giving the country its second successive win, part of a winning streak that saw Ireland win three years in four – all the talk the next day was about *Riverdance*.

It was such a sensation that it prompted Doherty and her husband

John McColgan to develop it into a two-hour stage show, which opened in Dublin in February 1995. It then alternated between Dublin and London, playing to packed houses for nineteen weeks at the Apollo Hammersmith. From there, it went around the world. It has been performed on every continent except Antarctica and been seen by an estimated 25 million people worldwide.

Following a series of disputes between Flatley and the producers, he left the show in late 1995. He was replaced at short notice by Colin Dunne, who made a considerable success of what many believed to be a poisoned chalice: Flatley just seemed an impossible act to follow. He in his turn went on to develop a number of similar shows of his own.

Riverdance opened in New York in early 1996. Its success there – first at Radio City Music Hall and subsequently at the Gershwin Theater on Broadway – anchored its international reputation. Although both Anúna and Jean Butler left the company, in 1996 and 1997 respectively, followed by Colin Dunne in 1998, the show was able to recruit able replacements. By now, there were a number of companies performing the show in different parts of the world. The interval act had become an international phenomenon.

Little Museum of Dublin

Until 2011, Dublin was the only capital in Europe without a city museum. There had been a venerable Dublin Civic Museum in a fine eighteenth-century building in South William Street. It was jointly curated by the Dublin Corporation and the Old Dublin Society, a voluntary body formed in 1934. However, this museum closed in 2003, leaving a huge gap in the city's infrastructure.

This gap was filled by the Little Museum when it opened eight years later. It was the brainchild of Trevor White, a magazine publisher and writer, and Simon O'Connor, a graphic designer and musical composer. There were problems: specifically, they had no building, no money and nothing to display.

Dublin City Council solved the first problem by leasing them a landmark Georgian building on the north side of St Stephen's Green. This has always been the most fashionable side of Dublin's most fashionable square: in the eighteenth century it was known as Beaux Walk, where young persons of fashion paraded, the better to see and to be seen.

They made a public appeal for artefacts. The results were astonishing, a great cornucopia of little treasures, memorabilia, bric-a-brac, old photographs, half-forgotten advertisements – just about anything that recalled the city's past. They received solid support from a number of major city businesses and professional practices: the goodwill that lay behind all this itself illustrated the gap that the Little Museum was designed to fill. In all, they now have more than 5,000 artefacts. Among the donors are members of U2, the novelist John Banville, Christ Church Cathedral and the family of the late writer Christy Brown.

In one of the smaller rooms, the museum has recreated the office of the legendary editor of the *Irish Times*, R.M. (Bertie) Smyllie, just as it was in the 1940s, even down to the great man's typewriter, desk and chair.

The Little Museum of Dublin opened in 2012. That year, it had 24,248 visitors. In 2015, this had more or less quadrupled to 101,076. In all, more than 267,000 visitors have crossed its threshold. Along the way, it has won plaudits and awards galore. On Trip Advisor it has been rated as the number one museum in Ireland – not just in Dublin. In just a few years, this remarkable institution is running at close to capacity.

As well as welcoming visitors in ever growing numbers, the museum hosts lectures and concerts, exhibitions and conferences, book launches and similar events and runs an active educational programme for schoolchildren, more than 9,000 of whom have benefited to date from this initiative, for which of course there is no charge. All this from a standing start in a few years.

At the time of writing, it has an option to buy the matching adjacent Georgian house from the Dublin City Council and is attempting to raise the necessary funds. This would provide the

Little Museum with a hugely impressive double-fronted classical building in a premium location, to facilitate the growth and further development of the collection and provide the city with a world-class facility. Whether it could still call itself the 'Little' Museum is a moot point, although the name is now an established brand. It would be a nice problem to have.

U2

First they were known as Feedback. Later they were called Hype. But the name that they finally settled on, U2, had the simplicity of being readily understood in any language. It was suggested by Steve Averill of Radiators From Space, a short-lived contemporary Irish rock group.

The band dates from 1976. It was founded by four schoolfellows at Mount Temple School on the north side of Dublin. The same four are still together: Paul Hewson (Bono), vocalist; David Evans (the Edge), lead guitar; Adam Clayton, bass guitar; and Larry Mullen, drums.

In 1978, they won a talent contest in Limerick: this brought them to the attention of Paul McGuinness, who became their manager. He first heard them play at the Project Arts Centre in Dublin and he developed them into one of Ireland's greatest success stories – and the one with arguably the longest cultural reach, given the immense popularity and critical acclaim they have enjoyed.

It was, perhaps inevitably, a slow start. The first EP was issued in 1979 and four singles in 1980 but they sold poorly. Their debut album *Boy* appeared in 1980, followed by *October* in 1981, each to positive notices. But neither was a commercial success. However, their fortunes turned decisively for the better in 1983, with the release of their third studio album, *War*, and U2 *Live: Under a Blood-Red Sky*. These albums moved them towards the first rank of rock bands. In 1984, their fourth studio album, *The Unforgettable Fire*, reached number 1 in the UK album charts.

Their songs were admired for their social concern and their political commitment, all of which secured them a loyal fan base. While the albums were selling well, what really stood to U2 by the mid-1980s was their success on the road. They became one of the top international touring bands. Crucially, they acquired a large following in the United States. All this was topped by the 1987 release of *The Joshua Tree*, the album that catapulted them into the showbiz stratosphere. *Rattle and Hum*, released to accompany the movie of the same name, followed in 1988.

In 1991 came *Achtung Baby*, an album that represented a reduced emphasis on social and political matters and introduced a fuller musical and showbiz palette. They promoted it on the road, with the Zoo TV Tour. The albums continued to flow through the 1990s, with a continued exploration of musical and artistic possibilities. No one ever accused them of resting on their laurels. *Zooropa* (1993) was followed by *Pop* (1997) and in 1998 a compilation album – a certain sign that they were now one of the world's biggest acts.

In 2000, U2 greeted the millennium with *All That You Can't Leave Behind*, which many regarded as a return to mainstream rock values. This critical opinion was consolidated by *How to Dismantle an Atomic Bomb* (2004). The band has continued to tour and to promote social and political causes to which they are devoted. Bono, in particular, has been highly visible in this regard internationally, having been photographed with everyone from the Pope to the President of the United States to Nelson Mandela. He is an instantly recognizable international celebrity.

The band has won numerous awards over many years, a testimony to their staying power but also to their talent for artistic redirection. More prosaically, all four of them plus McGuinness were made honorary freemen of the city of Dublin in 2000.

U2 STUDIO ALBUMS

Boy (1980)
- Hit single – 'I will follow'
- Charts – Number 52 in UK and number 63 in US

October (1981)
- Hit single – 'Fire'
- Number 11 in UK and number 104 in US

War (1983)
- 'Sunday Bloody Sunday' and 'New Year's Day'
- Number 1 in UK and number 12 in US

The Unforgettable Fire (1984)
- 'Pride (In the Name of Love)'
- UK and US Top 5

The Joshua Tree (1987)
- 'With or Without You'
- Number 1 in UK and US

Rattle and Hum (1988)
- 'Desire'
- Number 1 in UK and US

Achtung Baby (1991)
- 'The Fly'
- Number 1 in UK, number 2 in US

Zooropa (1993)
- 'Numb'
- Number 1 in UK and US

Pop (1997)
- 'Discothèque'
- Number 1 in UK and US

All That You Can't Leave Behind (2000)
- 'Beautiful Day'
- Number 1 in UK, number 3 in US

How to Dismantle an Atomic Bomb (2004)
- 'Vertigo'
- Number 1 in UK and US

No Line on the Horizon (2009)
- 'Get On Your Boots'
- Number 1 in UK and US

Songs of Innocence (2014)
- 'The Miracle (Of Joey Ramone)'
- Number 6 in UK and number 9 in US

Conor McGregor

McGregor is one of those phenomena that almost defies description or definition. He is to mixed-martial arts fighting roughly what Ryanair is to European air travel. He defines an entire sport, by far its biggest champion, biggest draw and biggest earner. He holds world titles at two different weights, welterweight and lightweight, an achievement unique in MMA history. Previously he had held the featherweight championship. He is a champion trash talker. Conor McGregor is showbiz gold.

Not bad for a lad from the working-class suburb of Crumlin in south-west Dublin. He was early attracted to boxing – the skill that is his strongest MMA suit – and first took up mixed martial arts at the age of 18. After a short amateur career, he turned professional in 2008 at the age of 20. Within five years, he had signed for the Ultimate Fighting Championship (UFC) based in Las Vegas. The UFC is the biggest promotion company in the sport. Its champions are de facto world champions.

MMA permits a mixture of fighting techniques to be employed – boxing, kick-boxing, ju-jitsu and so forth. It developed in the 1990s in a declared context of no rules, anything goes. This has been minimally modified over time to ban the more egregious practices but it is still seen by many as the Wild West of sport. Some American politicians have called for it to be banned altogether. Indeed, it was banned in New York State until early 2016. However, once the ban was lifted the UFC could stage promotions in the state. The contest in which McGregor defeated Eddie Alvarez to secure the lightweight title was held in one of New York City's most iconic venues, Madison Square Garden.

On his way up – he has been defeated only three times in twenty-four contests – McGregor has not been shy about letting the world know his opinions. Speaking of the featherweight division as he made his way in it, he noted that 'the division is full of rookies and has-beens ... I'm enjoying myself collecting these cheques on my way to eliminating each one.' On his success in the division: 'It was never about the champion. It was about me destroying every one of those featherweights and essentially make it a one-man division.' He is self-possessed to a remarkable degree: 'At the end of the day you have to feel some way. You may as well feel unbeatable, like a champion.'

He may not be unbeatable but he is a champion through and through.

Mrs Brown's Boys

If ever there was a case of 'everyone hates it except the public', *Mrs Brown's Boys* is it. A runaway success in terms of television ratings, it is scorned by many critics. One wrote that he 'would rather throw [himself] on top of a funeral pyre than watch *Mrs Brown's Boys*', although allowing that the programme 'was not commissioned with bitter cranks like me in mind', which redeems him somewhat. The *Guardian* hated it. Another simply judged it 'the worst sitcom ever made', none of which stopped it being voted the best sitcom of the twenty-first century in a UK online poll.

It is a vehicle for the considerable comic talent that is Brendan O'Carroll. For years, he beat around the Irish pub and club comedy circuit, relentlessly and unapologetically lowbrow, and carved out his niche accordingly. Well, it is not a niche any longer. O'Carroll first developed the character of Agnes Brown, played by himself in drag, in the early 1990s. He played her on stage, radio and straight-to-DVD movies. There were a number of books, originally published in Ireland, which later went international in the wake of the sitcom.

In the early 2000s, O'Carroll took the stage show touring in the UK. One night in Glasgow, a BBC producer went to see the show, acting on a tip-off from an actor he knew. He described the scene: 'The audience was full of old women laughing, alongside ushers who were sixteen or seventeen and also pissing themselves. It was immediately clear: there is something happening here.' The timing was fortuitous, as it always is in these matters: the BBC were concerned that their comedy offerings were too metro-liberal and anodyne, so Mrs Brown's raw, red-meat comedy might just prove an antidote.

BBC Scotland commissioned the first sitcom series in 2009, with RTÉ joining as co-production partner. It opened on RTÉ on 1 January 2011 and on BBC a few weeks later, on 21 February. Two more series followed quickly, plus Christmas specials. The public could not get enough of it. It won many awards, including a BAFTA, and was the most-watched television programme in the United Kingdom on Christmas Eve and Boxing Day 2014. On Christmas Day, an ordinary episode of the sitcom secured the highest ratings. A feature film, Mrs Brown's Boys D'Movie, appeared in 2014.

Mrs Brown's Boys makes no apology for itself, nor does it need to. It is certainly in many respects a throwback to a coarser form of comedy – with its innuendo-laden end-of-the-pier humour. Although of Irish provenance, it appeals to a tradition that had become submerged: that of honest British smut. It is a very clever product, carefully tailored to its target audience, written and acted by a formidably intelligent and focused man.

Brendan O'Carroll has a reputation for a sound business head, reviewing all his draft contracts himself. The character of Agnes Brown is based on his mother, Maureen O'Carroll, the first ever woman elected to Dáil Éireann for the Irish Labour Party. She subsequently became chief whip of the party. She was tough and courageous, an outspoken socialist at a time – 1950s Ireland – when the 's' word was not entirely respectable. Well, her son is not entirely respectable and he has done very well out of it. The fruit did not fall far from the tree.

19
WHIMSY

Leprechauns

The best-known of all Irish fairy creatures. A leprechaun is represented as a diminutive shoemaker, whose wealth is measured by his crock of gold. His uniform is a green coat and a scarlet cap. He is an elusive fellow and he needs to be, because if a human catches sight of him and then manages to keep him in sight, the leprechaun is obliged to hand over the crock of gold. Leprechauns pop up here and there in literature, most notably in James Stephens' *The Crock of Gold*, a comic fantasy novel published in 1912 which James Joyce – always sparing in his praise of other writers – admired.

JJ&S

Joyce's admiration for James Stephens (c.1882–1950) was such that he even considered a collaboration with him if, due to his failing eyesight, he was unable to finish *Finnegans Wake* unaided. The idea was that the book would then be entitled JJ&S (James Joyce and Stephens), a pun on John Jameson & Son, the well-known distillers. Today, this whiskey is ordered as simply a Jameson or a Jemmy but in Joyce's day a customer might indeed order a JJ&S.

Irish Juries

There are many variations on this theme, which suggests a perverse verdict of not guilty. In his book *The Old Munster Circuit* (1939) Maurice Healy (1887–1943) tells of a county court judge who addressed a prisoner thus: 'You have now been acquitted by a Limerick jury, and you may leave the dock without any further stain on your character.' In another variation on the theme, the judge said: 'Prisoner at the bar, you have pleaded guilty to a dastardly crime, but a jury of your own countrymen, who know you better than I do, have declared that you are an incorrigible liar. You are discharged!'

The Cúpla Focal

Irish for 'the couple of words', this is shorthand for the obligatory phrase in the grand old tongue delivered by a person with no further proficiency in the language. Irish is officially the first language of ROI although the reality is that Ireland is an anglophone country. Irish is a compulsory school subject to the end of second level, so everyone has the *cúpla focal* but for many people that's it. Politicians, in particular, are notorious for cranking out a few ritual words in Irish and then continuing in English.

Irish Bulls

An Irish Bull is an expression that is self-contradictory or absurd. It was originally a term of colonial condescension aimed at Gaelic speakers trying to express themselves in a new language. However, it was Sir Boyle Roche (1743–1807), himself a member of the ascendancy and an MP in the old Irish parliament, who is credited with more Bulls than most. Some examples of his linguistic mangling: 'Mr Speaker, I see a rat. I see him floating in the air and darkening the sky but I will nip him in the bud.' 'It would surely be better, Mr Speaker, to give up not only a part but if necessary the whole of our constitution to preserve the remainder.' And perhaps the most famous of all: 'Why should we put ourselves out of our way for posterity, for what has posterity done for us?' He then clarified this statement by explaining that by posterity he did not mean our ancestors but those who came immediately after them.

GUBU

It stands for grotesque, unbelievable, bizarre, unprecedented. In the summer of 1982, a double murderer called Malcolm MacArthur was arrested in the apartment of the then attorney-general. The lawyer, a family friend, was completely unaware of MacArthur's actions or situation but naturally the affair caused a sensation. The four words were spoken by the beleaguered Taoiseach, Charles J. Haughey, in response to the discovery. Conor Cruise O'Brien, who detested Haughey, used the words to form the acronym GUBU, which he then gleefully applied to all Haughey's subsequent bungles and misfortunes. It entered the public lexicon of Irish life.

The Pope's Brass Band

In the wake of the Great Famine (1847–52), a group of Irish MPs at Westminster came together in an informal alliance and called themselves the Irish Brigade. Because of the delicate parliamentary balance, they were in a position potentially to extract concessions from the government. They were opposed to the Ecclesiastical Titles Act (1851), legislation which forbade Roman Catholic dioceses in Great Britain to be named for any of the ancient church sees, which were reserved for the Established Church. In opposing the legislation, the Irish Brigade acquired the nickname of the Pope's Brass Band. The group fell apart when two of their number, John Sadleir and William Keogh, accepted public office. It did them no good. Keogh later became a judge and ended his own life in Germany by cutting his throat (1878). Sadleir also died by his own hand, on Hampstead Heath (1856) after a bank he owned failed and he was discovered to have overdrawn his own account by the colossal sum of £200,000.

Wear a Condom, Just in Casey

In 1992, it was revealed that the charismatic and media-friendly Bishop of Galway, Eamonn Casey, had fathered a child in 1974 with Annie Murphy, an American divorcee, while he was Bishop of Kerry. He had subsequently 'borrowed' £70,000 from diocesan funds to pay her off. The whole thing was regarded as hilarious, although there was a degree of public sympathy for the bishop, who was dispatched to South America for his pains. T-shirts bearing the slogan soon appeared on sale and one distributor of condoms renamed his business Justin Casey. Later church scandals elicited less mirth.

Take Her Up to Monto

Monto was short for Montgomery Street in Dublin's north inner city, the centre of the city's notorious red-light district. The ballad 'Take Her Up to Monto' is full of late Victorian references and slang, which led many to suppose that it was a contemporary composition. For example, there are references to W.E. 'Buckshot' Forster, Chief Secretary of Ireland from 1880 to 1882, and to Queen Victoria, who is celebrated in the final verse:

> The Queen she came to call on us / She wanted to see all of us
> I'm glad she didn't fall on us / She's eighteen stone
> Mister Me Lord Mayor, says she, is this all you've got to show
>   to me
> Why, no ma'am, there's some more to see: *póg mo hone*.

(The last phrase *póg mo hone* translates as 'kiss my arse'.)

Far from being a piece of late Victorian bawdy, the ballad was composed by George Hodnett, the jazz critic of the *Irish Times*, in 1958 and popularized by the Dubliners.

INDEX

A Note About the Author

Richard Killeen is an author and publisher based in Dublin. Among his previous works are The Concise History of Modern Ireland and Ireland in Brick and Stone.